GOD IN THE OPEN

COLOSSIANS AND PHILEMON

A Devotional Commentary

Ron Unruh

Ron Unruh

Copyright © 2016 by Ron Unruh. All rights reserved.

No part of this publication may be reproduced, stored in a retrieval system, or transmitted in any form or by any means, electronic, mechanical, photocopy, recording or otherwise without the prior written permission of the author with the exception of brief quotations and with exception as provided by Canadian copyright law.

Unruh Publishing

ISBN 978-0-9939342-0-9

All scripture quotations, unless otherwise indicated, are taken from the HOLY BIBLE, NEW INTERNATIONAL VERSION®. NIV®. Copyright ©1973, 1978, 1984 by International Bible Society. Used by permission of Zondervan. All rights reserved.

Scripture marked ESV is taken from the ESV" Bible (The Holy Bible, English Standard Version"), copyright © 2001 by Crossway Bibles, a publishing ministry of Good News Publishers. Used by permission. All rights reserved."

Christian Books / Reference / Commentaries / New Testament

Religion & Spirituality / Spirituality / Devotionals

Religion & Spirituality / Spirituality / Devotionals

Acknowledgement

I dedicate this book to Dr. Kermit Ecklebarger who was New Testament professor at London College of Bible and Missions and later at Ontario Bible College (now Tyndale University College) during my undergraduate years. He joined the faculty of Denver Seminary in 1972 and was appointed associate academic dean in 1991. He served as director of the doctor of ministry program from 1991 to 1994. He was the vice president and academic dean of Denver Seminary from 1993 to 2001 and senior professor of New Testament. Dr. Ecklebarger has continued to teach on-line courses and he serves on the D.Min. Committee for the Seminary. Dr. Ecklebarger and his wife Shirley live in Redmond, WA. He inspired an interest to understand New Testament revelation and to believe the content. More than any teacher or professor I have known, Kermit has sought to stay in touch with my classmates and me, shown interest in our work, and he and Shirley have become friends for whom we will always be grateful.

Table of Contents

Preface

Chapter One   I'M TALKING TO GOD ABOUT YOU ALL OF THE TIME (Col. 1:1-14)

Chapter Two   I'M TALKING TO YOU ABOUT GOD (Col. 1:15-23)

Chapter Three   THE MYSTERY OF GOD IS CHRIST HIMSELF (Col. 1:24-29 & 2:1-7)

Chapter Four   FALSE TEACHING CAN OBSCURE THE REVEALED MYSTERY (Col. 2:8-23)

Chapter Five   YOUR NEW IDENTITY COMES WITH NEW POWER FOR CHANGE, (Col. 3: 1-17)

Chapter Six   MOTIVATED TO PLEASE THE LORD WITH LIFE CHANGES (Col. 3:18 – 4:6)

Chapter Seven   A FAREWELL FROM PRISON (Col. 4:7-18)

Chapter Eight   THE RUNAWAY SLAVE, ONESIMUS (Philemon verses 1-29)

Preface

Colossians is often cited as a favourite New Testament letter. The text informs us that Paul and Timothy were responsible for this correspondence with the Church in Colossae. The authenticity of the letter is universally defended. Although a few scholars, in favour of an unknown follower of Christ, have challenged Paul's authorship, I write with the belief that Paul was the primary author. Paul's letters to churches were foundational to the establishment of early Christian theology. A doctrinal section and a conduct section appear as two distinct parts of this letter. Paul speaks to his concern that false teachers are spreading untruths with regard to both doctrine and conduct. The author therefore proclaims Christ's supremacy over the entire created universe and then he insists that believers must lead godly lives.

Colossians contains intriguing personalities and interpersonal relationships. Paul identifies a man named Epaphras as a dear fellow servant. "One of you," is the way Paul described him, and we gather that Epaphras was likely the founder of the church in Colossae. Onesimus is also spoken of as "one of you," an accepted brother and someone whom Paul valued as a personal helper. Dissimilar as they were, both Epaphras and Onesimus were Christians and Colossian residents. Onesimus was given the significant responsibility of delivering Paul's letter to Colossae. While this may seem a small task, it must be understood that Onesimus was once a slave. That's right. He was a slave to another Colossian named Philemon, a wealthy slave owner. Onesimus stole from Philemon and ran away but while he was absent he received Christ as his Saviour. Philemon too was a Christian. Because that relationship warranted a letter from Paul to Philemon that was incorporated into the canon of scripture, I have included it as the final chapter in this series from Colossians. The letter to Philemon follows so naturally.

I have written this book as a devotional commentary so that it may be useful to both students and teachers of the Bible. I have a two-fold objective. I want to provide information that will vitalize the individual follower of Christ who is reading for the purpose of personal growth. I also want to provide exegetical material to someone fashioning a lesson or a sermon. This twin intention is natural to me after several decades as a preacher and pastor and also as an adjunct teacher of homiletics. As I examine sections of the letters to Colossians and to Philemon, I present a creative interplay of factual information and my interpretation and application of the text. For those reasons there is admittedly a sermonic flavour to the writing. I always believed that a preacher should be the first one to benefit from the discovery of truth during the study time. I also think that any believer, though inexperienced with the original biblical languages, should find benefit by reading a commentary such as this. I point to the larger Pauline themes and examine the theological content in light of its original socio-cultural and historical contexts. Using a narrative style, I develop both the first century setting of Paul's letters to Colossians and Philemon and the relevance of the teachings for us in our day using illustrations that reflect our times and issues. I do not hesitate to point readers to personal invitations to belief and practice that naturally flow from the Pauline statements to readers who share the faith of the earlier Christians to whom these letters were first written. I emphasize the continuity of this literature as correspondence. I refrained from inserting footnotes or endnotes, opting rather to give credit within the text itself. I trust that you will find value in this recitation and explanation of the Biblical text.

Chapter One

I'M TELLING ON YOU

I'm Talking To God About You All Of The Time

Communication today is immediate but it is also unrefined since we have abandoned the art of letter writing. We are virtually paperless, seldom composing a hard copy letter or using the postal service. Cursive handwriting is almost dead. New technologies have forever changed our written communications. Software generates letter templates and auto-correct features require little thought about expression, style, and vocabulary. Via handheld devices we instantly text our messages and using social media platforms we convey our faces, activities and sentiments to a controlled group or to the world. Email messaging arrives with the sender's name, email address, subject line and time of sending to one person or to several. E-communication has limited inbox life, routinely being sent to trash after first read. There is little that is memorable. So there is both an upside and a downside to our communication capability today.

The hard copy letters of J.R.R. Tolkien, the letters of Earnest Hemingway, the letters of Thomas Jefferson, the letters of John Keats, and the letters of Vincent Van Gogh are collections of handwritten correspondence that have been valued and preserved. The writers are celebrated. Paul's letter to Colossians is a keeper too.

A Personal Blessing

The New Testament book of Colossians was a personal letter from Paul and his ministry colleague Timothy, addressed to the gathering of Christians in ancient Colossae. This first century communication has been conserved and read by people such as Thomas Aquinas, John Calvin, C.S. Lewis and you and me. It was correspondence worth keeping from someone who cared. It is also esteemed as inspired by the Spirit of God. Paul intended his letter to be shared with Laodicean believers nearby (Colossians 4:16). The correspondence follows a style of letter writing that was common to the first century Middle Eastern Graeco-Roman society. Written on parchment and rolled for easy transportation it looked very different from the paged letter within our Bibles. The title, the paragraph divisions and headings did not exist in Paul's draft but have been supplied by book publishers for the convenience of readers.

Upon receipt of the letter, a church member would have scrolled open the document and read it aloud to others announcing the cordial salutation from Paul and Timothy.

> *1 "Paul, an apostle of Christ Jesus by the will of God, and Timothy our brother, 2 To God's holy people in Colossae, the faithful brothers and sisters in Christ: Grace and peace to you from God our Father."* (Colossians 1:1,2)

Paul never travelled to Colossae himself. While the Colossians may have heard about him, they almost certainly had never met him. The ascriptions Paul applies to himself and to Timothy were important to establish credibility. He calls himself an apostle of Christ because he must introduce himself suitably if he expects the recipients to read and to accept his letter. Timothy is identified as *"our brother"* and that would be understood as a Christian term for 'fellow Christian' because Paul ascribes the same term to all of the Colossian believers when he calls them *"brothers and sisters"*. They belong to the same family of followers of Jesus, and Paul regards them as holy and faithful people to whom he extends this blessing. *"Grace and peace to you from God our Father."* As early as the first century, Christians would bestow benediction statements on one another. Perhaps we might revive this practice, adding as a tagline to a note or email message these several sanctifying words, *"Grace and peace to you from God our Father."* It sounds antiquated but it may be appreciated and it may be precisely what someone needs to hear.

The city of Colossae was located in a country known as Phrygia, now modern Turkey, and it was positioned one hundred miles east of the coastal city of Ephesus. The apostle Paul spent two years planting a church in Ephesus and Acts 19:10 tells us that radiating from that center, *"This went on for two years, so that all the Jews and Greeks who lived in the province of Asia heard the word of the Lord."* Some of Paul's converts engaged in missionary activity, fanned out from Ephesus and eventually a church was planted in Colossae. It is probable that a native of Colossae named Epaphras, who had learned the gospel from Paul in Ephesus, founded the Colossian church. From Colossians 1:21 we deduce that the church was composed mainly of Gentiles who knew nothing about the Judeo-Christian deity. *"Once you were alienated from God and were enemies in your minds because of your evil behavior,"* Paul reminds them.

Colossae was one of three important Christian cities known as the Tri-cities, the other two being Hieropolis and Laodicea. The cities were nestled in the Lycus River Valley where the Lycus River flowed through fertile acreage amid majestic mountains. This was on a major trade route in Roman times. Great flocks of sheep were produced on this pastureland, making it a lucrative centre for the wool industry and for woolen garments. Colossae was specially known for dark red wool called Colossinum. Laodicea was the financial and political hub and Hieropolis was known for its spas and medicinal mineral waters. Over time, this gentile, Phrygian, Turkish country became populated by Jewish families moving to the region for the baths and the wines and the business opportunities. They prospered and by 62 B.C. the Jewish population was as high as 50,000. To this multi-cultural people the gospel of Jesus Christ came. Many people became Christians and house churches began in all three cities.

Constantly Thank God for Other Believers' Faith and Love

Paul heard about the Colossian believers from Epaphras who had taken the gospel to his fellow citizens in Colossae. Paul's perception of the believers in Colossae was that the gospel, like well planted seed, had produced good fruit among them.

> *3 "We always thank God, the Father of our Lord Jesus Christ, when we pray for you, 4 because we have heard of your faith in Christ Jesus and of the love you have for all God's people— 5 the faith and love that spring from the hope stored up for you in heaven and about which you have already heard in the true message of the gospel 6 that has come to you. In the same way, the gospel is bearing fruit and growing throughout the whole world— just as it has been doing among you since the day you heard it and truly understood God's grace. 7 You learned it from Epaphras, our dear fellow servant, who is a faithful minister of Christ on our behalf, 8 and who also told us of your love in the Spirit."*
> (Colossians 1:3-8)

Since Epaphras told Paul that these people were living consecrated and authentic lives, Paul, as a God ordained apostle of Christ wrote to them, telling them that he prayed for them. The section of verses 3-8 is actually one single protracted sentence in Greek, containing this opening disclosure that Paul regularly prays for the recipients even though he has never met them directly. In my own amplified version of verse 3 and 4, I hear Paul saying, *"When we pray for you, we always give thanks for a couple of primary reasons. When we pray for you, we repeatedly thank God because (1) you trust in Jesus Christ and (2) you love Christians everywhere."*

That you trust in Jesus Christ may seem like a rudimentary first reason for which to be giving prayerful thanks but I view it as sincerely vigorous. My wife Christine and I have five grandchildren. When we ourselves were young parents, we were diligent to provide our children with enough information for them to believe in Jesus. We wanted them to understand the information and to make a responsible decision to believe that God sent his son Jesus into the world to become a ransom for sinners, which by virtue of our human natures, we all are. Our understanding was and is that by trusting in Christ, we can become God's spiritual children with the prospect of being with God in heaven when this life is done. Now we have five grandchildren, and we feel that a hands-on transmission of truth is one generation removed. We are not with these children every day. Our grandchildren have parents of their own who have primary responsibility for their spiritual nurture. Nevertheless, Christine and I desire to know that these five precious people will know Christ personally. We pray for them now, looking forward to the day that we can pray with buoyant thanks that each of one of them trusts Jesus. That will be a great day. Paul was saying here, *"We frequently thank God because you trust in Jesus Christ."* "Frequently" or "always" is synonymous to, "thank you, thank you, thank you, thank you."

You may spend a lot of time thinking about one or two loved ones. Whether or not that loved one of yours is doing everything right, if you are able to thank God that this loved one is trusting in Jesus, you are a happy person. When you pray for this person, start here. "Thank you Lord that so and so trusts in you." Then carry on from there with your requests for the development, the improvement, and the correction you discern is needed in that person's life. It's a fantastic first reason for thanksgiving and Paul was letting Colossians know that he was thanking God all of the time for their trust in Jesus. The first thanksgiving note is faith.

The other reason for which Paul gives thanks, is the Colossians' love for all the other Christians or saints. Such love for all believers was an evidence of spiritual renovation in their lives because their hesitations to love everyone, whether social or theological, were downgraded when pure love concentrated upon what they all had in common with others, namely Jesus Christ.

I have witnessed a demonstration of this noteworthy feature within the Canadian socio-political arena. Ideological tensions between French-speaking Quebec and the rest of English-speaking Canada have sometimes become headline news. Within the Christian community however, such strain is suspended from both cultures when they meet because of love between believers. Their commonality of faith in Christ proves to be superior to political attitudes.

Ideally that's the way that believers should relate to one another but the history of Christianity reveals occasions when Christians have become tribalistic, allowing theological differences to polarize them. Two groups may believe in Jesus, but concerning baptism, or Christ's second coming, or the Holy Spirit, or women in church leadership, the two tribes disagree and each tribe believes the other is wrong, and each criticizes and avoids the other because they don't want cross pollination. Paul would find that reaction distasteful.

A deliberate shift away from such exclusivity was made within western Christianity during the past quarter century. This was exemplified when at Trinity Western University in Langley, British Columbia, the Trinity Western Seminary established a model for disassembling tribalism. The seminary was founded by the Evangelical Free Church of both Canada and the U.S.A., a group of autonomous churches whose ethos is summarized by the distinguishing statement, "In essentials, unity; in non-essentials, charity; and in all things, Jesus Christ." That freedom encouraged the EFC to identify other groups who loved Jesus, like the Christian and Missionary Alliance, Pentecostal Assemblies of Canada, Fellowship of Evangelical Baptists, Canadian Baptists and Mennonite Brethren and to invite them to partner in creating a consortium called ACTS, Associated Canadian Theological Schools. This association shares expertise, resources, faculty and experiences and together these partners prepare and educate vision-filled Christian leaders to meet needs within this changing world. This is a demonstration of love for all God's people.

Paul makes a noteworthy alliance between these two thanksgiving notes of faith and love. When a person places faith in Jesus Christ there is a natural corollary that follows; there's an affinity for others, a loving relationship with others who have also believed in Christ. Paul knew this from personal experience, because prior to meeting Christ, he despised Christians and their faith and he persecuted them. After Christ confronted him, Paul became a champion for Christianity. As Paul matured spiritually and travelled, he recognized that the Roman world was exceedingly secularized, making it very important for Christians to know that they were not alone, not isolated. They needed to have confidence that in the next town there were other disciples of Jesus who loved them. This was reciprocal, mutually supportive, and emboldening.

When Paul elaborated about faith and love in verse 5, he mentioned to these believers the concepts of hope and heaven and gospel. Here is what he said. *"The faith and love that spring from the hope stored up for you in heaven and about which you have already heard in the true message of the gospel."*

That this hope is reserved in heaven for you is not a hypothetical notion or a matter of conjecture but rather the Bible makes reference to heaven and Jesus spoke about heaven as authentic. We likely do not study or talk enough about heaven. It's nearer than any of us know. Christian music has sometimes conveyed notions of heaven that are intended to reduce the perceived distance between here and there and between now and then. One song entitled 'Finally Home,' with lyrics by L. E. Singer and music by Don Wyrtzen contains the refrain, "But just think of stepping on shore and finding it heaven; of touching a hand and finding it God's; of breathing new air and finding it celestial; of waking up in glory and finding it home." It suggests heaven as a familiar and welcoming venue where the LORD is waiting with open arms to receive you into this incredible ambiance of God's glory that will now be your home.

It is in verse six that Paul reminds these Christians that upon hearing the gospel and understanding the undeniable grace of God, spiritual fruit was produced among them and that fruit has kept growing. Paul quickly adds that this same gospel is similarly bearing fruit and growing among people worldwide. It's a global occurrence, not a phenomenon, because it is to be expected when God's gospel is proclaimed and received. The old gospel standard says, "Just as I am without one plea, but that thy blood was shed for me. And that thou bidst me come to Thee. O Lamb of God I come." The gospel, with its invitation to forgiveness and to new life has been fruitful in every generation. No wonder that for a season of time in great stadiums around the globe, God used Billy Graham, together with that refrain sung by baritone, George Beverly Shea, to call to saving faith large numbers of people who stepped from their own pasts as they watched other strangers doing the same, and to entrust their lives to the same good news gospel to which Colossians responded two thousand years earlier. Immediately among these converts there was this love for one another like a blanket comforter enveloping a stadium of people. Faith and love form an alliance.

Colossian believers had learned the truth of the Gospel from a faithful messenger named Epaphras who in Colossians 4:13 is identified as being from their city. *"Epaphras, who is one of you."* I already suggested the likelihood that Epaphras was the founding evangelist of the Colossian church. His name was a shortened version of Epaphroditus, which derives from Aphrodite, the Greek goddess of love, and that suggests that the man may have come from pagan background to become a convert of Paul. Paul loved this dear faithful minister and fellow servant. While Paul was under house arrest in Rome between 61-63 AD, it was Epaphras who visited him and told Paul about the Colossian problem about which we are yet going to learn and he stirred Paul to write this letter.

Persistently Pray that Other Believers will be Spiritual Winners

In verses nine through fourteen, Paul announces that he prays for these Christians. Here he tells them that from the first time that he heard about them, he has regularly and without fail been praying to God for them and he has been making specific requests of God concerning them. Remember what he already has written. He heard about their faith in Christ and their embrace of the gospel and of their lock on heaven and their love for believers. So for that reason he is asking God for several things pertaining to them.

> *9 For this reason, since the day we heard about you, we have not stopped praying for you. We continually ask God to fill you with the knowledge of his will through all the wisdom and understanding that the Spirit gives, 10 so that you may live a life*

> *worthy of the Lord and please him in every way: bearing fruit in every good work, growing in the knowledge of God, 11 being strengthened with all power according to his glorious might so that you may have great endurance and patience, 12 and giving joyful thanks to the Father, who has qualified you to share in the inheritance of his holy people in the kingdom of light. 13 For he has rescued us from the dominion of darkness and brought us into the kingdom of the Son he loves, 14 in whom we have redemption, the forgiveness of sins.* (Colossians 1:9-14)

I had a colleague who as a Director of Prayer Ministries, championed prayer among churches, inspiring them to prioritize prayer. His example elevated the importance of prayer for me and now in my volunteer service as chair of our district of churches, I schedule our board members to spend substantial time in prayer before we even try to do any business. We need God. We find that decision-making is expedited and we make wise decisions.

I am weary of hearing about churches that have imploded. Far too frequently, relationships between church members or between pastors and church boards become adversarial. Disputes are routinely juvenile, squandering all the good that has been accomplished over several years. And then we pray, desperate post-traumatic prayer for relief, for forgiveness, for revival. So late, perhaps in some cases too late! Why not pray in advance to intercept satanic assaults upon the health of congregations? Our district board, to which I have already referred, has begun to pray pre-emptively, preventively, and proactively. We want to interrupt wickedness before it germinates or grows. That's what Paul was doing by praying for the Colossian Christians constantly. Such consistent preemptive intercession can be applied to individuals, family members and friends.

Around the world people of various faiths use some form of prayer.

Christian Science devotees pray. So do Wiccan witchcraft enthusiasts. Dutiful Muslims face Mecca five times each day to pray a ritualistic prayer that is commanded in the Quran and then they follow that with personal requests. Hindus engage in meditation and prayers with rituals and chantings to deities. Attentive Jews pray three times a day according to prayers outlined in the Siddur or Jewish prayer book containing a set order of daily prayers. By the way, the Siddur is now available for iPhone, Blackberry and Androids.

Having recognized the universality of the prayer concept, it is crucial to understand that **it matters to whom a person prays**. A lot of prayer worldwide falls on deaf ears. The exercise of prayer itself affects nothing unless the prayer is directed to the person who can answer prayer, that is, the one true and supreme creator God. Not all prayers ascend to him. Here is a classic story to illustrate the distinction.

In ancient Israel, a prince named Ahab succeeded his father on the throne and by the age of 38 he had committed more evil acts than any predecessor. He married a woman named Jezebel who introduced him and his nation to the Phoenician cultic worship of Baal. Baal is a term that means master and lord and refers to any god. This however was a specific Baal whom Ahab worshiped and for whom Ahab built a temple with an altar. This was a violation of God's command and it was offensive. This Baal was nothing more than a statue. Elijah was a prophet of God and he made the declaration to Ahab that Israel was not going to receive another drop of rain or even dew for several years until Elijah himself would say so. Jezebel began a systematic extermination of all of the prophets of God that she could find. Elijah was hidden and he survived.

Three years later when the drought was severe, Elijah came to

Ahab to say that God would send rain. First however, Elijah demanded that the 450 prophets of Baal meet him on Mount Carmel to do a reality show. Baal's prophets were told to slaughter a bull, carve it in pieces, which they would lay on an altar of wood, but they should not ignite the wood. Instead they were to pray to Baal. Elijah said he would carry out the same steps and call on the LORD, the god who answers with fire. The prophets of Baal began in the morning to call on Baal and by noon they were shouting to him but no one answered. They danced around the altar as they screamed Baal's name, and now Elijah had a little fun with them. "Shout louder. Perhaps he's deep in thought, or he's busy, or he's gone on a trip, or maybe he's sleeping and you'll have to wake him up." They increased the volume and even in desperation began to cut themselves, which was a customary display of cultic devotion. Then it was night and no deity had paid attention to their pleading. Baal was silent! Time was up. Elijah called everyone to his altar that he had constructed with twelve stones, one for each tribe of Israel, and he dug a deep trench around it. On the altar he placed the meat of a second bull. He had four large jugs of water poured over the offering and the wood. He repeated that a second and third time until the trench was filled with water. Then Elijah prayed.

When he finished praying, fire from the LORD fell and burned the sacrifice, the wood, the stones, the soil and every drop of water in the trench. The people, seeing this, all fell down and prostrated themselves and cried out loudly, *"The Lord, he is God! The Lord, he is God!"* Soon the sky grew dark with clouds, the wind increased, there was the sound of approaching heavy rain and then it poured. It truly mattered to whom Elijah prayed and the people woke up to that reality.

Old Testament history chronicles numerous people who knew that it mattered to whom they were praying, so they prayed to the LORD God,

Jehovah, the God of creation and incredible results occurred. They were people such as Abraham, Jacob, Moses, Hannah, Elisha, David, and Solomon. Okay, so the lesson is obvious, but you and I live in the year 20-something, and the world is different than it was in those early centuries. Potable water flows through pipes and comes out hot or cold at the turn of a tap. Water can come steaming through a Keurig or a Kitchenaid and deliver latte or dark roast coffee. Fire is a Bic flick away, and the Weber or Microsave or wood-burning oven will cook a pizza or a steak perfectly. Thirty miles doesn't take three days but thirty minutes. Communication does not wait for weeks or months but the gap of time between Send and Receive. I have no impulse at the moment to pray like Elijah and I have no confidence that I can pray like Elijah. The crucial takeaway here is that God listens to our prayer.

Walk with me through this string of queries. Have you already made the faith commitment that acknowledges that Jesus is the only begotten Son of God who came from the Father to become a ransom? By means of that redeeming act, do you believe that sinful creatures which we naturally are, can be transformed through a spiritual rebirth to become new creatures in whom God's Spirit lives? Because you know yourself to be child of God, do you look forward to dwelling one day with God in his Holy Place for eternity? In this interval between now and then, God permits us to converse with him. Maybe our correlation with prayer comes down to this. How much of a difference do you want to make in this world? How much do you want to see God's kingdom come?

Moe Norman was a Canadian golfer, whom some say suffered from autism. That's possible because he had societal challenges and his speech was sometimes confusing, but on the autism spectrum he was likely a genius, certainly as far as the biomechanics of his golf swing were concerned. He developed a unique uncomplicated swing with a simple grip. He won scores of Canadian golf championships but never made it in the PGA past a couple of appearances in the Master's tournament. Professional golfers in any decade including Michelson, Woods, and Zach Johnson still today say he was likely the most accurate striker of the ball that has ever played. People who have heeded his advice have knocked 20 strokes off their game because they learned to hit straight, time after time. Do you want to play? How well do you want to play? Even now you can purchase recorded golf instruction by Moe Norman.

Do you want to pray, and do you want to pray effectively? If we truly want to talk with God, to pray, it's helpful to hear someone pray. It is even advisable to listen to someone whose prayers have made a difference. Jesus used prayer throughout his entire life. Everything that he did, whether it was confronting people, teaching people, healing people, resisting temptation, defying the devil, maintaining his spiritual stamina was done in conjunction with prayer. If we could only hear him pray to the Father it would be so informative for us. Jesus is identified with three prayers, the Lord's Prayer, The High Priestly Prayer and the Gethsemane Prayer. In those three prayers, Jesus explicitly instructs us how to talk to God, and he also models it himself at the most critical times of his life. By praying, Jesus, the God-man, set an example for fellow Jews and all of his followers for all time, while also maintaining unbroken solidarity with his Father.

If we were to spend several earth days with Jesus, observing why he prayed, when he prayed, for whom he prayed, and where he prayed, we would be strides further down the road to spiritual maturity. Well we can't do that. He has come here and gone. We are here now. He is coming back but it's only to escort us home if we have not already made the transition by the time he arrives. In the meanwhile, wouldn't it glorify God and make life pleasant if a few more of us could overcome addictions, chemical dependency, porn, anger and a few other assorted scourges? Wouldn't it glorify God and make life exciting if some of our neighbours and family members came to know Jesus personally? Wouldn't it glorify God and make life worthwhile if we saw each day as a fresh opportunity to see how God was going to use us? Prayer makes such things happen. God makes such things happen. We need to talk with him. How much of a difference would you like to make? If you want to play, you follow a golf master. If you want to pray you follow the advice and the example of the master Jesus Christ.

When you think of some of the people for whom you have the deepest love, or the utmost concern, isn't your desire for them to know and to understand God's will? If you are thinking of a person who has not seen a need to repent of personal sin and to place complete trust in Jesus Christ, you want that person to understand that according to God's program, Jesus came and surrendered himself to a death that was substitutionary in the place of us all. If you are thinking of a child or a youth whom you want to see spared the common mistakes and blunders of the growing and adolescent years, you want them to understand God's will for them. Pray! And don't stop praying.

You and I can never use the excuse that we don't know how to pray for someone. Here is an example of prayer that can pretty much cover anyone whom we know. Again, think of your father or mother, or brother or sister, or grandparent, or close friend, or school friend, or neighbour and then consider praying like this.

"Dear Father in heaven, I am asking that you fill Ron with the knowledge of your will so that he will live a life that is worthy of

you and will please you in everything he does or says. Lord give him such a great understanding of your will and make him spiritually wise so that his work has outcomes that you regard as good fruit. May he be constantly growing in his knowledge of you. Strengthen him with your power so that he will have unassailable perseverance and unflappability. May he rejoice before you because he knows that his sins are forgiven and he has been redeemed because you have rescued him from the darkness that dominated him and you have qualified him and brought him into your Son's kingdom of light. Amen.

You may even pray for yourself.

"Lord, I want to live a life that honours you so I am asking that you will make me spiritually wise, that is, please teach me to know and to understand your will. If you will help me to know your will, then I know I can please you in everything, bearing fruit in how I spend my time, getting to know you better, being empowered with your power so that I can resist and be strong and be patient. And thank you for redeeming me and forgiving me of my sins and lifting me from the dominion of darkness and giving me admission into Jesus Christ's kingdom of light with all other believers."

Chapter Two

ETERNAL, INVISIBLE

I'm Talking To You About God

Imagination is integral to my craft as a painter. Suppose that I consider painting a picture of God, not as an idol to be worshipped but rather to tell God's story using visual imagery, how can I paint God when God is not observable? I am confounded. God is concealed, invisible. I have no model, nothing upon which to base a rendering. However, I remember that Jesus was a young adult when prayed the words, "our Father who lives in heaven." Imagination encourages me to envision God the Father as at least one generation older than Jesus himself. Furthermore, in first century culture, men did not shave their beards so God likely had a long white beard. Would that seem plausible? It's highly unlikely. Let's say that it's at least convenient because it indulges the human mind that finds it easier to process the physical than the spiritual. The famous Italian artist Michelangelo had no hesitation in painting a representation of God on the ceiling of the Sistine Chapel in Rome. In his central scene of creation, Michelangelo painted God as a Caucasian white-bearded grandfatherly patriarchal figure extending his forefinger in a gesture by which he was imparting life to a newly created Adam. That was pure speculation and it was likely gloriously incorrect because no one has seen God the Father and the Bible says that God is spirit and we cannot assume God looks like a man. In fact the task of painting God is more problematic than any of us might imagine.

I often play orchestral classical music while I paint. As I begin to paint my proposed portrait of God, let me suppose that I stimulate my creative ability by listening to one of the great hymns of the previous century, a Welsh tune by John Roberts (1839) with lyrics written by Walter Chalmers Smyth (1876), entitled, 'Immortal, Invisible, God Only Wise.' The result might be that I become so absolutely mesmerized by the person of God, so enthralled in the worship of the incomprehensible, invisible God that even imagination couldn't help me to paint God. I am in an even greater quandary than when I began. Listen to the words and consider how could we possibly paint a portrait of this?

> *Immortal, invisible, God only wise,*
> *In light inaccessible hid from our eyes,*
> *Most blessed, most glorious, the Ancient of Days,*
> *Almighty, victorious, Thy great name we praise.*
> *Great Father of glory, pure Father of light,*
> *Thine angels adore thee, all veiling their sight;*
> *All laud we would render: O help us to see*
> *'Tis only the splendour of light hideth thee.*

Almighty God Made Himself Visible in Jesus

The biblical evidence is clear that Jesus is God and that he came in the flesh to show God to us. The mysterious invisibility of God has always been a problem for humanity. The seeming invisibility of God is where agnostic and atheist thinkers make their mistake by equating invisibility with unknowability and from that conclusion, then leaping to God's non-existence. However, scientists have long ago learned that invisibility is not equivalent with imaginary or pretend or untrue. Science knows that atoms are invisible but they are real. So are sound waves, time, wind, and gravity invisible but nonetheless existent. God's Invisibility does not make God less authentic, less authoritative, less nearby. Rather, this breathtaking, invisible God is as actual as anything else that we perceive with our senses. The wind blows wherever it pleases and it makes things happen, like waving grasses and bending trees and crashing waves at the shoreline. Similarly God affects outcomes. He exists even though he is unseen.

With this painting predicament, I turn to Colossians 1:12-20 and specifically verse 15 where I find a most profound resource.

> *12 ... and giving joyful thanks to the Father, who has qualified you to share in the inheritance of his holy people in the kingdom of light. 13 For he has rescued us from the dominion of darkness and brought us into the kingdom of the Son he loves, 14 in whom we have redemption, the forgiveness of sins. 15* ***The Son is the image of the invisible God, the firstborn over all creation****. 16 For in him all things were created: things in heaven and on earth, visible and invisible, whether thrones or powers or rulers or authorities; all things have been created through him and for him. 17 He is before all things, and in him all things hold together. 18 And he is the head of the body, the church; he is the beginning and the firstborn from among the dead, so that in everything he might have the supremacy. 19 For* ***God was pleased to have all his fullness dwell in him****, 20 and through him to reconcile to himself all things, whether things on earth or things in heaven, by making peace through his blood, shed on the cross.* (Colossians 1:12-20)

Two truths are stated in verse 15. **First**, God is invisible, and **second**, Christ reflects and reveals God. *"The Son is the image of the invisible God, the firstborn over all creation."* We cannot find God by searching for him because we don't know where to look or for what to look, but if God reveals himself to us, then we can know him according to that revelation. Humanity either concludes that God does not exist or it fabricates unverifiable notions about God. Stated again, unless the real God reveals himself, which is what God has done, humanity cannot know God.

It is the Son of God who is the ultimate subject of this section. Publishers of the Bible, not Paul, inserted paragraph divisions as a convenience to readers. In verses 13 and 14 Paul wrote that God rescued believers and brought them into the kingdom of his Son whom he loves.

Editors have used a highlighted heading and created a break between verses 14 and 15 that effectively interrupts Paul's developing, continuing thought about Christ's supremacy. That interruption compels us to note that in verse 15, although the "Son' is not repeated in the original language, it is the Son who is the implied subject of the statement, *'He is the Image of the invisible God.'* The son is the natural, logically deduced subject within this context. The NIV has supplied what the original text and the other translations inferred which is, *"The Son is the image of the invisible God ..."*

The disciple named John spent a lot of time with Jesus, heard him, witnessed miracles, listened to him pray and in John's personal testimony he wrote, "In the beginning was the Word, and the Word was with God, and the Word was God. He was with God in the beginning. Through him all things were made; without him nothing was made that has been made," and, *"The Word became flesh and made his dwelling among us. We have seen his glory, the glory of the one and only Son, who came from the Father, full of grace and truth,"* and, *"No one has ever seen God, but the one and only Son, who is himself God and is in closest relationship with the Father, has made him known."* (John 1:1-3,14,18). In coming here, Jesus made God visible to us. Jesus is God.

On the night before His death, Jesus responded to Philip's request, "Lord, show us the Father and that will be enough for us," by saying, "Don't you know me, Philip, even after I have been among you such a long time? Anyone who has seen me has seen the Father. How can you say, 'Show us the Father'? Don't you believe that I am in the Father, and that the Father is in me? The words I say to you I do not speak on my own authority. Rather, it is the Father, living in me, who is doing his work." (John 14:8-10)

Scripture is God's self-revelation. There is so much in scripture that attests to Jesus being God and coming in flesh to make God known and to let people see God face to face. When Jesus was here, he proclaimed, "*I and the Father are one*" (John 10:30), by which he meant "of one essence or nature." Only "God" can be of the same nature as "God".

With verse 15 informing me, I know that if I can paint Jesus Christ, I have nailed my purpose to paint God. Jesus is after all, the image of the invisible God who is spirit, or is spiritual in nature. If I paint Christ, I have painted the person of God. As satisfying as it may be for me artistically to know that if I paint Christ, I have painted a portrait of God, Paul wrote this statement not to give Colossians artistic inspiration but rather to correct some wrong headedness about Jesus.

Jesus is Dependably Preeminent

The city of Ephesus was on the coast of the Aegean Sea, and 100 miles east and inland were the Tri-cities of Colossae, Laodicea and Hieropolis. The seed of a church at Ephesus was likely planted when some Ephesian people returned from Jerusalem where they had gone to worship during the Festival known to us as Pentecost. The Day of Pentecost about which Acts chapter two speaks, was the day when the disciples of Jesus were demonstrably filled with the Holy Spirit and they publicly proclaimed the gospel in many unlearned languages. Hearing this good news, thousands of people put their faith in Jesus that day and then returned to their homes throughout the Roman Empire. Presumably a few converts returned to Ephesus.

Paul visited Ephesus on a couple of occasions, the last time staying there for three years from 54-57 AD. In 62 AD, perhaps five years after

Paul departed from Ephesus for the last time, he was placed under house arrest in Rome. This was a great hardship for him but he was given permission to receive visitors. One of those visitors was Epaphras, a Colossian man with a pagan background who had become a Christian conceivably when he heard Paul speak in Ephesus. He may have been among the many Jews and Greeks of the province who attended Paul's instruction in the hall of Tyrannus (Acts 19:8-10). After his conversion, Epaphras became a teacher of the gospel and helped to establish a church in Colossae. Epaphras brought encouraging news to Paul about the progress of the churches in the region, but he also reported a strong tendency among the Christians in Colossae to embrace false teachings. Heretical teaching was posing a threat to the Colossian church and Gnosticism was the most dangerous heresy. Concerned that the Christians might turn from the true gospel, Paul wrote this letter to the Colossians. Gnostics were questioning the sufficiency of Christ and the supremacy and humanity of Christ. Now we can understand Paul's concern. The Colossian believers might become confused about God and Christ and their faith and security. We should have similar concern for professing Christians of our day who either do not understand God and Christ well, or are at risk of becoming confused by inferior teaching and theology. And if Christians who should be salt and light may have their faith shaken, how will the tens and hundreds of thousands of people who need Jesus, be presented with a convincing introduction to him.

In Israel today, where Jesus lived two millennia ago, 50% of the population is secular or irreligious, with 37% agnostic and 15% atheist. Jesus is far from their thoughts. He is certainly not immediate to the minds of North Americans. 76% of Americans identify themselves as Christians, with 51% being Protestant and 25% Roman Catholic, 4% other religions including Judaism, Buddhism, Islam, and Hinduism and another 20% with no religions affiliation (American Religious Identification Survey (ARIS) of 2008). At least half of the professing Christians in American do not regularly attend any church. It's a nominal association. Of the Canadian population 67% is Christian with a Catholic majority; 24% have no religion and Islam has 3.2% of the population. Religious adherence is steadily decreasing.

Sincere Christians must have our act together. We have to be convinced about Jesus. In this letter Paul establishes the complete sufficiency of Christ, both for salvation and sanctification. Jesus is unquestionably all you need for salvation and he is undeniably all you need to become a godly person. God took upon Himself flesh so we could "behold" Him. This was the point of the angels' words to Joseph concerning the upcoming birth of Jesus; "*...and they shall call His name Immanuel', which translated means 'God with us'*" (Matthew 1:23). Secularized Jews don't believe that, nor do practicing Jews who are still waiting for a Messiah.

Paul's commanding thought in this section of verses is 'the Preeminence Of Jesus'. There are many secular and philosophical notions today that try to erode Biblical data about Christ. Paul's teaching speaks to Christ's incomparable supremacy by featuring aspects of his Lordship.

Jesus Is Lord Of Creation

*15 The Son is the image of the invisible God, the **firstborn over all creation**. 16 For **in him all things were created**: things in heaven and on earth, visible and invisible, whether thrones or powers or rulers or authorities; **all things have been created through him and for him**. 17 **He is before all things**, and **in him all things hold together**. 18 And he is the head of the body, the church; he is the beginning and the firstborn from among the dead, so that **in***

> ***everything he might have the supremacy.** 19 For God was pleased to have **all his fullness dwell in him**, 20 and through him to **reconcile to himself all things**, whether things on earth or things in heaven, by making peace through his blood, shed on the cross.* (Colossians 1:15-20)

Jesus is God and in coming here, he made God visible to us and Paul presents Jesus as firstborn, or LORD OF CREATION. In making the statement that Jesus is the firstborn over all creation, Paul started with the suffix 'proto' meaning 'first,' or 'foremost,' and that could be fitted to a number of Greek terms just as we do in English to indicate precedence or primacy or priority. The English word 'prototypical' is the first of its type so it is archetypal, perfect, exemplary. Here Paul selected a word that would best refute heresy, so he did not use the Greek term "protoktizo" which means 'first created,' because he wasn't created but instead Paul chose "prototokos", meaning 'first born.' Jesus was born but he was exceptional, something like the eldest child in that ancient culture being in a position of preeminence over his siblings.

To demonstrate Jesus' exceptionality, his primacy, Paul tells us the astounding truth that, the one who came like this, is the one who at the beginning of earth time created everything. Paul calls Jesus "*the firstborn of all creation*" and says, "*by him, all things were created.*" And Paul uses this 'all creation' and 'all things' theme seven times in verses 15-20 to hammer home that Jesus is absolutely supreme.

> *15 The Son is the image of the invisible God, the firstborn over **all creation**. 16 For in him **all things** were created: things in heaven and on earth, visible and invisible, whether thrones or powers or rulers or authorities; **all things** have been created through him and for him. 17 He is before **all things**, and in him **all things** hold together. 18 And he is the head of the body, the church; he is the beginning and the firstborn from among the dead, so that **in everything** he might have the supremacy. 19 For God was pleased*

> to have all his fullness dwell in him, 20 and through him to reconcile to himself **all things**, whether things on earth or things in heaven, by making peace through his blood, shed on the cross. (Colossians 1:15-20)

Jesus is dominant. This means that Jesus created a Christ-centred universe, things in heaven and on earth, visible and invisible, whether thrones or powers or rulers or authorities. All things were created by him and for him. He was to have supremacy over every created thing. We shouldn't rush past this but rather we should be struck with the marvel that Jesus, who walked in Palestine in century one is the same person who created the entire earth, set within its enormous expanding universe home. I wish so much that residents of Israel understood this. I wish that residents in my housing complex understood this.

We impress ourselves with our genius in this digital age when we humans have been able to fit thousands of books into a tiny chip. If there was ever a question about Christ's preeminence, then consider that our universe generates comets which as they move they exhale vapor trails that may be 10,000 miles long yet if all that vapor could be bottled, it would condense into only a cubic inch of space. Jesus made them. These verses tell us that Jesus created Saturn whose rings are 500,000 miles in circumference, but only about a foot thick. Jesus made the earth to rotate around the sun eight times faster than the speed of a bullet shot from a gun, yet we are hardly aware of this rotation. Among the many insect species that Jesus created, he made bees and programmed them so that when seasonal heat threatens to melt the wax inside a bee hive, bees become their own air conditioner by fluttering their wings at the entrance and inside to create a cross draft that pushes out hot air and draws in cooler air. Jesus created the human chromosome to contain 20 billion bits of information which if written in hard copy books would be the equivalent of

4000 volumes.

And Jesus who preceded everything by virtue of being eternal and making everything for himself, also holds it all together and sustains it (verse 17).

Themes of creation dominated the first part of this passage (Col. 1:15-17) and themes of redemption dominate the second half (Col. 1:18-20). At verse 18 we can identify another emphasis about Christ's preeminence.

Jesus Is Lord of The Church

Jesus not only was the agent who created all that exists, but he is also the agent of our salvation.

> *18 And he is the **head of the body, the church**; he is the beginning and the firstborn from among the dead, so that in everything he might have the supremacy. 19 For God was pleased to have all his fullness dwell in him, 20 and through him to reconcile to himself all things, whether things on earth or things in heaven, by making peace through his blood, shed on the cross.* (Colossians 1:18-20)

These two programs, creation and redemption, are side-by-side, but in between them historically is something that explains why Christ's business needed to be *"to reconcile to himself all things."* Humanity fell away from God, broke solidarity with God through sin, and the only way for the disharmonies of nature and the inhumanities of humankind to be resolved; the only way for the harmony of the original creation to be restored and for peace to be reestablished between humans and God, would be if a human made things right, that is, atoned for that sin. That atonement was settled on the cross of Christ when the blood of the one who is the image of the invisible God, the Son himself, was shed as he died. Quite simply put, Jesus made it all, and then Jesus paid it all, in order for us to have a relationship with the living God.

But Jesus did not remain dead. Verse 18 says, "*He is the head of the body, the church. He is the beginning and the firstborn from among the dead...*" Paul uses that word 'firstborn' again. Jesus is the beginning of something else, a great long parade of people who will also rise from the grave as he did but Jesus is the firstborn of us all, and that entire crowd is called 'The Church.' Jesus is Lord of the Church; the head of the Church as befits his preeminence, because after all, everything that God is, was pleased to dwell in Jesus when he was here on earth. Verse 19 says, "*For God was pleased to have all his fullness dwell in him.*" When Paul used the term 'fullness' like this, it meant the totality of God with all his powers and attributes was invested in the incarnate Son of God. Paul is saying in effect, that the divine fullness is at home permanently in the Lord Jesus. It's nothing that has been added to supplement him but rather it is part of his essential nature, his constitution. Jesus is God. He is preeminent and he is therefore Lord of the Church.

There have been others who were raised from the dead before Jesus. They came to life, yes. But they were incapable of staying alive. In the town of Nain to which Jesus and his disciples had travelled, they were observed a funeral procession for a young man, the only son of his widowed mother. When Jesus saw her so heartbroken, he was moved in his heart and said to her, "*don't cry*". At the same time he touched the coffin carrying her son's body and announced, "'*Young man, I say to you, get up!' The dead man sat up and began to talk, and Jesus gave him back to his mother.*" (Luke 7:11-14)

Elsewhere, the family of sisters Mary, Martha and their brother Lazarus was special to Jesus. Their home in Bethany was his home when he visited. Jesus was several days walk away from Bethany when word came to him that Lazarus was very ill. Had he started out right away he might have arrived before Lazarus died, but he remained where he was for two more days and meanwhile Lazarus died, although the disciples were not yet aware of that news. The entire story is told in John 11:1-44. The disciples could not understand Jesus at the time, and admittedly, he did say curious things like, *"This sickness will not end in death. No, it is for God's glory so that God's Son may be glorified through it."*

Jesus also told his disciples, "Our friend Lazarus has fallen asleep; but I am going there to wake him up."

When he and the disciples arrived, the town of Bethany was in mourning and Martha met Jesus and said sorrowfully to Jesus, *"Lord, if you had been here, my brother would not have died."*

Jesus said them, "Your brother will rise again."

Martha answered, "I know he will rise again in the resurrection at the last day."

Jesus said to her, "I am the resurrection and the life. The one who believes in me will live, even though they die; and whoever lives by believing in me will never die. Do you believe this?"

"Yes, Lord," she replied, "I believe that you are the Messiah, the Son of God, who is to come into the world."

When Jesus was shown the sealed cave where Lazarus' body was entombed for four days, he commanded attendants to move the large stone from the entrance. Martha was immediately concerned that there would be an offensive odor of decay, to which Jesus replied, *"Did I not tell you that if you believe, you will see the glory of God?"* Then Jesus prayed. *"Father,*

I thank you that you have heard me. I knew that you always hear me, but I said this for the benefit of the people standing here, that they may believe that you sent me."

Then Jesus called into the dark mouth of the tomb, "*Lazarus, come forth,*" and the man rose and shuffled out, still bound by the strips of burial cloth in which he had been laid to rest in peace days before.

Here is the decisive point. Both the widow's son and Lazarus were resurrected to life but not with resurrection bodies. Life returned to their physical bodies. Theirs were the same physical bodies that would still be subject to illness and eventual death. Jesus, however, was the first to rise from death in a resurrection body. During the forty days that followed his resurrection, Jesus was able to appear, materialize as it were, in the presence of his disciples. They could touch him, feel him, and then he could vanish. That body was distinctively different from Lazarus post death body. Christ's was a resurrection to life that is forever, and it is to this that all believers have been given promise. That's why in 1 Corinthians 15:20, Paul called Jesus the firstfruits of those who have fallen asleep. Jesus is the first one of all those who die in faith, who like Jesus will also rise again to life that lasts forever. He is the beginning. So Jesus is the head, he's supreme in the church in Colossae and everywhere else since he is the one upon whom it depends. He is preeminent.

An entire section of 1 Corinthians chapter fifteen speaks to this resurrection to which we look forward and counters arguments that some theorists and unbelievers make. It is of value to place Paul's rebuttal here.

> *12 But if it is preached that Christ has been raised from the dead, how can some of you say that there is no resurrection of the dead? 13 If there is no resurrection of the dead, then not even Christ has been raised. 14 And if Christ has not been raised, our preaching is*

> *useless and so is your faith. **15** More than that, we are then found to be false witnesses about God, for we have testified about God that he raised Christ from the dead. But he did not raise him if in fact the dead are not raised. **16** For if the dead are not raised, then Christ has not been raised either. **17** And if Christ has not been raised, your faith is futile; you are still in your sins. **18** Then those also who have fallen asleep in Christ are lost. **19** If only for this life we have hope in Christ, we are to be pitied more than all men. **20** But Christ has indeed been raised from the dead, the firstfruits of those who have fallen asleep. **21** For since death came through a man, the resurrection of the dead comes also through a man. **22** For as in Adam all die, so in Christ all will be made alive. **23** But each in his own turn: Christ, the firstfruits; then, when he comes, those who belong to him. **24** Then the end will come, when he hands over the kingdom to God the Father after he has destroyed all dominion, authority and power. **25** For he must reign until he has put all his enemies under his feet. **26** The last enemy to be destroyed is death.* (1 Corinthians 15:12-26)

Further to Christ's Lordship of the Church, and building upon the fact that all of God was in Christ, Colossians chapter one, verse 20 then says, *"And through him to reconcile to himself all things; whether things on earth, or things in heaven, by making peace through his blood, shed on the cross."* The disobedience of the first two humans infected the entire race so that harmony with God was forfeited. The penalty of death and decay was imposed on humanity and affected all of creation. Reconciliation was required and God has take the initiative to reconcile all things to himself through the Son, or by means of the Son, Jesus Christ, because Christ's death has made peace possible between God and Humans. When it speaks of *"all things"* being reconciled, we must interpret this in a manner that does not contradict other scripture. Reconciling "all things" must have qualification. Remember Colossians 1:12 when Paul gave thanks *"to the Father who has qualified you to share in the inheritance of the saints in the kingdom of light?"* Paul was saying this to Colossians who had qualified by trusting in the Lord Jesus. The qualification cannot be ignored. Unrepentant and unbelieving people and fallen rebellious angels are not included in the "all" category of things reconciled to God. The '*all things*' include people who trust in Christ. Everything will be resolved to God's satisfaction.

In the last verses of this section, Paul explains how the shedding of Christ's blood on the cross could make peace between God and everything else including us. It makes this next momentous point.

Jesus Is Lord Of The New Creation

Paul was writing to Colossian believers whose lives were transformed by Christ. Before the gospel was preached to them, they lived in isolation from God and their conduct and lifestyles displayed that they treated God like the opposition. When they received Paul's letter, they were completely different from what they were before the gospel was preached to them. The change occurred when they accepted by faith that Jesus is the Son of God who died to redeem them and make them saints and members of His body, the church, with the hope of heaven as a continuous prospect.

> *21 Once you were alienated from God and were enemies in your minds because of your evil behavior. 22 But now he has reconciled you by Christ's physical body through death to present you holy in his sight, without blemish and free from accusation— 23 if you continue in your faith, established and firm, and do not move from the hope held out in the gospel. This is the gospel that you heard and that has been proclaimed to every creature under heaven, and of which I, Paul, have become a servant.* (Colossians 1:21-23)

Recent to the time of Paul's writing, Colossian Christians had been entertaining thoughts that they were not good enough, or they had not done enough, or that Christ's part was not sufficient. They questioned whether their worship was good enough, or whether they had sacrificed enough? They were tempted to try to incorporate some Jewish or even pagan ceremonial works into their salvation. This was part of the heresy that worried Epaphras and Paul. They were forgetting the gospel that Epaphras had brought to them. They needed to be reminded why they had believed the gospel in the first place. It had been so compelling. Salvation did not depend upon them. They couldn't work their way into God's favour. The cross represented God's wrath against sin and Jesus willingly represented humanity when he died on the cross, absorbing that wrath himself according to God's plan, so that God could show love to us who trust the gospel story. Paul was exhorting them never to forget this. Don't trust anything that diverges from Jesus being central and preeminent. Verse 22 says, *"But now he has reconciled you by Christ's physical body through death to present you holy in his sight, without blemish and free from accusation."*

Do we need this reminder too? There are so many Christians these days having second thoughts about church, about the trustability of scripture, the need for the Old Testament, the emphasis on guilt and punishment. Are you among them? If Paul were here, he would say to us, "there is nothing more important to you than the gospel of Christ." You were dead and helpless and God intervened and he saved you through Christ. You can't add anything to the gospel, but surely don't try to subtract anything either. It is only through the death of Christ that you are blameless and God can regard you as his child.

Jesus will be faithful and he will present you blameless and holy in the presence of the Father, but verse 23 states a proviso, with "if." *"If you continue in your faith, established and firm, and do not move from the hope held out in the gospel."* As you persevere and stay solidly fixed, that is evidence of authentic faith that is guaranteed to result in the "well done, good and faithful servant" commendation you will receive in heaven. Not for a moment is Paul saying that genuine salvation can be lost or squandered or that salvation is not by grace alone but rather by some work. Persevering is not a work that can save you or keep you saved, but rather, persevering to the end reveals that you are genuinely saved.

Here's the thing. We either believe that we were alienated from God because of sin and that God used the death of his own Son to reconcile us to himself and to make us holy before him or we don't believe it. Only those who remain fixed and immovable on that foundation can enjoy this assurance. As I said, this is not a hint that salvation may be lost by Christians, but rather it is the acknowledgement that assuming you are unmoved by false teaching, the hope of the gospel still pertains to you. All true children of God do not get dislodged from that certainty.

"This is the gospel that you heard and that has been proclaimed to every creature under heaven, and of which I, Paul, have become a servant." Paul is saying in verse 23 that respect for him should keep them from being moved away from the gospel. This is the gospel I preach, he says. This is the gospel that you were told and it's the gospel that has been universally proclaimed because Christ commanded that.

Let me bring you back to Walter Chalmers Smyth's hymn lyrics, entitled, 'Immortal, Invisible, God Only Wise,' from which I earlier cited the first verse. Now here follow the remaining stanzas. It captures the majesty of the eternal, invisible, sovereign one whom Jesus fully displayed while he was invested with a human body for a few years of earth-time.

> *Unresting, unhasting, and silent as light,*
> *Nor wanting, nor wasting, Thou rulest in might;*
> *Thy justice like mountains high soaring above,*
> *Thy clouds which are fountains of goodness and love.*
> *To all life Thou givest, to both great and small;*
> *In all life Thou livest, the true life of all;*

> *We blossom and flourish as leaves on the tree,*
> *And wither and perish, but nought changeth Thee.*
> *Great Father of Glory, pure Father of Light*
> *Thine angels adore Thee, all veiling their sight;*
> *All laud we would render, O help us to see:*
> *'Tis only the splendor of light hideth Thee.*
> *Immortal, invisible, God only wise,*
> *In light inaccessible hid from our eyes,*
> *Most blessed, most glorious, the Ancient of Days,*
> *Almighty, victorious, Thy great name we praise.*

Now perhaps I will sit at my easel and seek to paint a likeness of Christ. Or, wait a minute, better than that, I will let him display his likeness through me.

Chapter Three

THE MYSTERY OF GOD IS CHRIST HIMSELF

Language is not always clear. Idiomatic English expressions can be misunderstood, specially by people for whom English is their second language. For instance, I could confuse people when I use expressions such as, 'a stitch in time saves nine; I have a frog in my throat; let's get down to the nitty-gritty; she's been cooking the books; he flies by the seat of his pants; look, no more love handles; she cried crocodile tears; you're a couch potato; we lived on a shoestring; let's bury the hatchet; quit beating around the bush; I survived by the skin of my teeth; I'm so hungry I could eat a horse."

You and I might struggle to understand Jamaican creole patois. "Suh yuh nah guh badda guh," means, "So, you are not going to bother going." Or try this one, "Ah sake ah ar mek eem nah lef yah" which means, "it's because of her that he's not leaving here."

Sometimes, even without a strong accent or cultural idiom, we can be misunderstood language when we do not say precisely what we mean. At times the writing of the apostle Paul has been misunderstood. As you read verse 24, doesn't it sound as though Paul was saying that with his own physical suffering he was completing something that was lacking in Christ's sufferings? Here it is within its context.

> *24 Now I rejoice in what I am suffering for you, and **I fill up in my flesh what is still lacking in regard to Christ's afflictions**, for the sake of his body, which is the church. 25 I have become its servant by the commission God gave me to present to you the word of God*

> *in its fullness— 26 the mystery that has been kept hidden for ages and generations, but is now disclosed to the Lord's people. 27 To them God has chosen to make known among the Gentiles the glorious riches of this mystery, which is Christ in you, the hope of glory. 28 He is the one we proclaim, admonishing and teaching everyone with all wisdom, so that we may present everyone fully mature in Christ. 29 To this end I strenuously contend with all the energy Christ so powerfully works in me.* (Colossians 1:24-29)

Paul's Puzzling Expression - Is Something Lacking in Christ's Suffering?

Surely he could not have meant that something was lacking in Christ's effective afflictions or suffering. Christ's afflictions were for the sake of his body, the church. We know that. We know Jesus was innocent. He was wrongly put to death. However, in God's plan, his death served as atonement for human sin because it was God the Son in a human body dying on the cross as a substitute. That sacrificial act, that indelible image, is the decisive faith factor. God conditions his forgiveness of our sins, and his promise of everlasting life upon our faith in Jesus and what he accomplished. Paul agreed with this theology and he would not have implied that his own suffering was fulfilling or completing what was lacking in Christ's suffering. Yet readers, students and teachers have discussed this and debated this possibility over many years, because Paul's language is imprecise. What did he mean?

I believe that Paul was simply suggesting that he was doing his share. The responsibility to spread the word about reconciliation with God rested on individuals whom God commissioned. Paul was a servant or minister of that gospel as he says in verse 23, "*This is the gospel that you heard and that has been proclaimed to every creature under heaven, and of which I, Paul, have become a servant.*" Then in verse 25 he says that he became a servant or minister for the body of Christ, the church, to make

God's Word fully known to these Colossians. The task as it turned out, necessitated suffering for Paul. Christ suffered for the church and now Paul suffered for the church in telling the church about Christ. This was not a presumptuous or boastful statement. Colossian believers knew that Paul was under house arrest and later in jail in the city of Rome. A Roman jail was not a place of comfort but rather a place of privation and hunger, cold and illness and loneliness. Paul was there because his mission in life now, was to tell people that Jesus Christ is himself the disclosure of the mystery of God. The term, 'the mystery of God' sums up the enigmatic nature of God to the human mind. Who is God? What are his attributes? What can God do and what does he do? Can we approach him? Can we communicate with him? Does he love us? Is he kind? Will he help us? What are his expectations of us? Those questions comprise the mystery of God but Jesus is that mystery revealed in a human form.

By the time Paul was an adult, Jesus had been dead and gone for many years. As a young man, Paul, whose former name was Saul, was a devout Jew, obedient to the Torah and waiting like everyone for the Messiah. Saul thought he had theology nailed down, only to learn during a dramatic event, that he had missed an essential of God's message. Acts 9:1-19 carries Paul's conversion story. Saul had been convinced that Jesus was a fraud. Saul felt that it was an insult to his Jewish faith and it was an offense to Jehovah that there were people who still trusted Jesus as their Messiah, so Saul gained synagogue authorization to punish Christians. Then Christ confronted Saul in a vision that was convincingly authentic by virtue of Saul being rendered blind from a blast of light and Christ asked Saul, *"I am Jesus whom you are persecuting but go into the city of Damascus and I will show you what to do."* His travelling companions could also hear the voice but saw no person and they escorted Saul to

Damascus. The blindness and the authenticity of the voice of Jesus were so traumatic for Saul that he neither ate nor drank anything for three days.

In Damascus there was a Christian named Ananias, to whom the LORD also spoke miraculously, instructing him to "go to the house of a man named Judas and there you will find a person called Saul who will be prayerfully waiting for you. He is expecting someone named Ananias whom he has seen in a vision that I gave him, and he has seen that Ananias will touch him and restore his sight." Ananias was initially shocked and replied that he had heard about Saul, that he was a nasty man affecting many evil acts against Christ's followers. The Lord answered, "I have chosen him to carry my name to Gentiles and kings and to the children of Israel and I am about to reveal to him how much he will have to suffer for the sake of my name."

Ananias obeyed and when he located Saul, he said, *"The Lord Jesus who appeared to you, has sent me so you can regain your sight and be filled with the Holy Spirit."* Saul was healed and fed and strengthened and he went into the synagogue and proclaimed that Jesus is the Son of God. He was so enthusiastic as he stated this, that within a few days the chief priests plotted to kill him. Paul escaped and went to Jerusalem and there he boldly preached in Jesus' name until the Hellenists also tried to kill him. This was the beginning of the opposition that Paul experienced as he began his gospel work and this opposition would continue throughout his short life and helps to explain his reference to personal suffering for the sake of the gospel.

God who is invisible came in human flesh in the person of Jesus Christ, that is, God the Son inhabited a human body to reveal God to humanity. That was always a decidedly unpopular message among Jews

God in the Open

who viewed Jesus as a heretic, and also among secularists who viewed Jesus as a nuisance and a political liability. Finally, Jesus was summarily tried, sentenced and put to death and the opposition felt they were successful in ridding themselves of Jesus, yet still the stories about him continued. For instance, the stories that Jesus was alive from the dead and that he had appeared numerous times to his disciples. Some stories were undeniably true. On that first Day of Pentecost that followed Christ's death, his outrageous disciples created a panic in Jerusalem, with their noisy nonsense that turned out to be genuine languages that the disciples had never learned. Non-resident Jews who were in the city for the festival, confessed to understanding the good news in their own languages and dialects and that audience resulted in mass conversions of people who believed. Years later, Paul and the people whom he had mentored, were still crisscrossing the landscape promoting this bizarre Jesus cult.

Even as he wrote this prison letter, Paul was suffering but he was also saying that he could endure because he knew that his suffering was a small contributing part in the big faith picture for Christ's body, the church that began because of what Christ suffered. If Paul must suffer in order to tell everyone that Jesus Christ is the mystery of God, then he rejoices in being able to do that. That's what Paul's perplexing statement conveyed but we should be even more certain.

Christ is the Mystery and Paul Suffers to Make that Known

Paul uses the term 'mystery,' the Greek 'musterion' (a hidden thing, a secret') on four occasions in this letter alone (Colossians 1:26, 1:27, 2:22, and 2:43.) Mystery in this sense was truth, doctrine, or hidden wisdom that was purposely concealed and hidden by God from past generations. Such mystery is never understood until God reveals it. It's spiritually discerned but never intellectually or religiously apprehended.

Clearly and openly declaring that Christ's afflictions had been for the sake of his body, the church was the responsibility of individuals whom God commissioned and Paul had been appointed by God to make God's Word fully known to these Colossians (1:25). Paul emphasizes that what these Colossians have become privileged to learn about God and Christ is really the mystery that has been concealed from people for ages, for generations, but God has chosen to disclose it now, and these Colossians are fortunate beyond words. Paul urges his letter recipients to put complete faith in Jesus Christ. Many of them had already done that and others were doing it even as Paul was writing this affirmation from his prison cell. No wonder he could say that he actually rejoices in his sufferings.

Because we can be convinced from what Paul said earlier, that Jesus' death was sufficient to reconcile us to God, I will return now to that confusing comment by Paul in verse 24 concerning his sufferings filling that which is lacking in Christ's afflictions. In order to get to the bottom of it, I will take you to the bottom of this paragraph of scripture and work backwards. Let's see what that exercise tells us. Here again is what Paul said, followed by the bottom to top summary of what Paul is saying.

> *24 Now I rejoice in what I am suffering for you, and I fill up in my flesh what is still lacking in regard to Christ's afflictions, for the sake of his body, which is the church. 25 I have become its servant by the commission God gave me to present to you the word of God in its fullness— 26 the mystery that has been kept hidden for ages and generations, but is now disclosed to the Lord's people. 27 To them God has chosen to make known among the Gentiles the glorious riches of this mystery, which is Christ in you, the hope of glory. 28 He is the one we proclaim, admonishing and teaching everyone with all wisdom, so that we may present everyone fully mature in Christ. 29 To this end I strenuously contend with all the energy Christ so powerfully works in me.* (Colossians 1:24-29)

The Strength for his proclamation - His proclamation concerns Jesus Christ. From where does Paul's stamina for this demanding responsibility come? In verse 29 Paul explains that he is endeavoring energetically with a strength that he attributes to Christ's power at work in him. *"To this end I strenuously contend with all the energy Christ so powerfully works in me."*

A Purpose for his proclamation - Paul's purpose for this intense labour is clearly stated in verse 28. Paul evident purpose is to bring people to spiritual maturity. *"He is the one we proclaim, admonishing and teaching everyone with all wisdom, so that we may present everyone fully mature in Christ."* Sometimes Paul admonishes and sometimes he teaches. The method depends upon the condition of the people to whom he speaks.

A Definition of the proclamation - A more explicit definition of what Paul is proclaiming to people is found in verses 26 and 27, that is, *"the mystery that has been kept hidden for ages and generations, but is now disclosed to the Lord's people. To them God has chosen to make known among the Gentiles the glorious riches of this mystery, which is Christ in you, the hope of glory."* The mystery exists not because it is impossible to understand but rather because it was hidden for so long. At the time of Paul's writing however, the mystery had been revealed to the saints. The riches of the glory of this mystery about God and his activities is Christ residing in Gentile people, living in you, he tells the Colossians. What was unrevealed for ages, was the fact that the Jewish Messiah, the Christ, would reach in grace to non-Jewish people and indwell them, live inside them, and give them the ancient promise of Abraham, that is, entry into the kingdom of God's Son, which is the hope of glory. That great mystery has been revealed and Paul is one of those who is proclaiming and teaching this everywhere, namely that the indwelling of the Messiah and the hope of the glory of God belong to everyone who trusts in Christ.

In verse 25 Paul is giving testimony that his proclamation of Christ is simply the fulfillment of a commission or stewardship given by God to Paul. He was called to serve God and to serve the church by spreading the gospel. *"I have become its servant by the commission God gave me to present to you the word of God in its fullness."* Paul was told to take the Word of God to the nations and to offer to them the hope of glory and invite them to believe it.

Now we are back at verse 24 where Paul tells the Colossians that this ministry of his, of making known to the nations the mystery of Christ and the hope of glory, teaching them and admonishing them, does involve personal suffering for Paul . *"Now I rejoice in what I am suffering for you, and I fill up in my flesh what is still lacking in regard to Christ's afflictions, for the sake of his body, which is the church."* Paul is doing his share. That's what Paul is saying. There is a cost to him personally and here is how is suffering fits with what Christ has done.

The Only Thing Lacking is Christ's Physical Presence

The summary of those verses informs us that what Paul meant was not that Paul's sufferings were adding anything to the worth of Christ's afflictions but rather were extending their worth to all of the people that they were meant to bless. Christ's afflictions were not deficient in any way in terms of worth or merit. They adequately cover the sins of all who believe. The infinite value of Christ's afflictions remain a mystery to most people, hidden in the world, and God's intention has always been that this mystery should be revealed, extended to Gentiles the world over. The world is a large place. People are scattered. So in that sense, the afflictions of Christ are lacking. What is lacking is the knowledge of those afflictions everywhere to everyone. Ministers of the Word must carry the benefit of Christ's sacrifice, and I am not talking about ordained pastors. Ministers are all of us who share good news with others and in so doing we fill up what is lacking in the afflictions of Christ by extending that information to others.

I feel strongly that this is what Paul was intending to say because he wrote something similar in his letter to Philippi. In Philippians 2:25-30 Paul was talking about his deep respect for Epaphroditus. Paul is sending the man back to the Philippian church so they will joyfully honour him. Here is his reason stated in verse 30, "*... for he nearly died for the work of Christ, risking his life to complete what was lacking in your service to me,*" (ESV). The NIV put it this way, "*because he almost died for the work of Christ. He risked his life to make up for the help you yourselves could not give me.*"

What was still lacking in the Philippians' service to Paul that the man Epaphroditus completed, or filled up? That may help us to understand what Paul meant when he made reference to something lacking in Christ's afflictions that Paul's suffering filled up? This is how we should understand it I believe. The gift to Paul was a gift from the church as a body. It was a sacrificial love offering. It may have consisted of money, supplies, and books. What was lacking was the church's personal presentation of this offering to Paul. They could not all be there. Both Paul and the Church would have loved to be together when he received their gift but that was impossible so that is the part that was lacking. Epaphroditus therefore supplied this lack by his own zealous service, travelling to Rome to visit Paul.

Similarly, Christ prepared a love offering for the world by suffering and dying for sinners. It is lacking in nothing as far as its effectiveness, but what it lacks is Christ's personal presentation of himself in every town and village and city and workplace and school in the ancient world and in our world. God's answer to this lacking ingredient is to call people like Paul, and like you, to present the afflictions of Christ to others all the way from Damascus, to Jerusalem to Vancouver, to Toronto and Montreal, to Bolivia and Ukraine and Haiti. In doing this, you and I fill up what is lacking in the afflictions of Christ. We finish that for which those afflictions were designed, which is a personal presentation of the infinite worth of the atoning death of Jesus Christ.

The way that Paul said this in verse 24 of Colossians chapter one is really important. He says that it is in his sufferings and his actual flesh, in his actual suffering body that he does his share of filling up the afflictions of Christ. People should recognize the suffering of Christ by the very example of the commitment of a church that is willing to suffer to deliver the news.

We Make Christ's Presence Real

The Huaorani people of the rainforest of Ecuador, commonly known by the pejorative term 'Auca' which means 'savages' came finally to know Christ personally through a remarkable display of the gospel. In 1956 Jim Elliot, Nate Saint, Ed McCully, Pete Fleming, and Roger Youderian were attacked and speared by a group of Huaorani warriors as the men tried to bring Christianity to the tribe. A few years later, Elisabeth Elliott, widow of Jim Elliott, and Rachel Saint, sister of Nate Saint, came to live in the Huaorani village to show revenge-free love. This eventually led to the spiritual transformation of many, including some of those involved in the killing and essentially eliminated tribal violence. By the afflictions which

God in the Open

they themselves experienced, the murdered men and these family members made the afflictions of the Saviour real.

My uncle Harry was 40 years of age when he died of complications of rheumatic fever, but during the weeks of his last hospitalization his demonstration of resolute hope in Christ and confidence about heaven spoke volumes of redemption to nursing staff. On one of his last days alive, he sang to two nurses, a Fanny J. Crosby song.

> *Safe in the arms of Jesus, Safe on His gentle breast;*
> *There by His love o'ershaded, Sweetly my soul shall rest.*
> *Hark! 'tis the voice of angels Borne in a song to me,*
> *Over the fields of glory, Over the jasper sea. Refrain:*
> *Safe in the arms of Jesus, Safe on His gentle breast;*
> *There by His love o'ershaded, Sweetly my soul shall rest.*

The happiest people in the world are the people who know the mystery of Christ as the hope of glory, and it satisfies them so much that nothing else takes precedence and they are freed to extend the sufferings of Christ to others regardless of the personal cost. That's what Paul meant in verse 24. "Now I rejoice in my sufferings for your sake."

God is calling us to live for the sake of the gospel even if it means doing it through suffering. Suffering didn't just happen to Christ. Christ chose suffering in order to create and perfect the church. God calls us to choose suffering too. Do you remember this comment?

> *"Then Jesus said to his disciples, "Whoever wants to be my disciple must deny themselves and take up their cross and follow me. For whoever wants to save their life will lose it, but whoever loses their life for me will find it." Christ's cross was for propitiation. Ours is for propagation. He suffered to accomplish salvation and we suffer to spread it. Our willingness to endure hardship is filling up Christ's suffering.* (Matthew 16:24,25)

Oswald Sanders was the general director of China Inland Mission, which later became Overseas Missionary Fellowship. He wrote over 40 books, even one book per year from age 70 to age 90 when he died. In his book 'Spiritual Leadership,' he told the story of an indigenous missionary who walked barefoot from village to village in India preaching the gospel. With many discouragements and through miles of hardships, he tried to speak the gospel but was rejected. After being thrown out of one village one day, he fell asleep under a tree outside the village. When he awoke, a crowd was gathered around him. They had seen his blistered feet and believed him to be a holy man and wanted to hear his message that he obviously was so desirous of sharing that he would suffer to do so. With his blistered feet he was filling up the afflictions of Jesus.

John Piper's book 'Let the Nations Be Glad: The Supremacy of God in Missions,' contains the story of a 1983 conference of itinerant evangelists, sponsored by the Billy Graham Association and held in Amsterdam. Joseph was an unlikely attendee, a Masai warrior whose story was so compelling that he was given the opportunity to tell it to Dr. Graham. Joseph was a tall and slender man whose face bore the ritual Masai scars received after killing a lion with only a spear and shield. Joseph was walking one day along a dirt road when someone met him and shared the gospel of Jesus Christ with him. He immediately trusted and Jesus became his Lord and Saviour. God's Spirit transformed his life and filled with enthusiasm, Joseph wanted to share the good news with the members of his local tribe. He went from door to door telling them that Jesus suffered and died on the cross for their sins. He expected that people would become enamored with this news like he had been. Instead they became violent and village men held him to the ground while women beat him with lengths of barbed wire. He was then dragged from the village to die in the bush. After managing to crawl to a water hole and after some days recuperating, he was able to stand and to walk. He determined to return to his village. But he wondered what could account for the hostile reception he had received from people he had known all of his life. Had he left out some essential factors or details to the story about Jesus? He rehearsed the message that had first learned and then he re-entered his village, limping through the circle of huts. He called out, "Jesus died for you, so you could be forgiven and come to know the living God." Once again he was seized and beaten, reopening his wounds. Then he was dragged unconscious from the town. He survived that second beating as well, waking up days later in the bush. He was more determined to go back and when he did, the townspeople attacked him again before he could even speak a word. As they were beating him unmercifully, he told them that Jesus Christ could forgive their sins. Then as he lost consciousness, the last thing he remembered seeing was that some of the women who were beating him, were weeping. When at last he woke again, he was in his own bed. His tormentors had become his nursing staff trying desperately to save his life. While he was unconscious, the entire village had decided to put their trust in Jesus Christ. When Joseph finished telling his story, he lifted his shirt to show the scars that covered his chest and his back. He thanked Dr. Graham for listening and he walked away. Billy Graham said to others in the room, "I'm not fit to untie his shoes, and he wanted to meet me?"

Perhaps now we can understand what Paul meant when he said, "*I complete what is lacking in Christ's afflictions, for the sake of his body.*"

There is an incredible seduction in the North American prosperity gospel proclaimers, telling people that nothing but good things and lucrative things and blessings and health and wholeness will be yours if you trust Jesus. Don't fall for it. It will throw you off. It will destroy your confidence in God when disappointments come. Instead, do not be moved from your faith no matter what, but be stable and steadfast, never shifting from the hope of Christ's gospel.

Bob Dobson, with whom I attended Bible College, entered the field of public education. Much later we became fellow pastors in the same church. Bob has always been a people person, a conversationalist, an evangelist. In June 2006 as he drove his wife, his mother, his daughter and son in law and a new grandchild on a vacation trip, his van was struck by an oncoming out of control vehicle. Bob's wife and mother were airlifted from the accident scene but died in a Portland, Oregon Hospital. The other three adults were broken to bits but the little boy was untouched. To date Bob has had thirty-four surgeries to allow him to move and to walk. What is most important about Bob is that through every moment of this lengthy and lifelong horror, his faith in Christ has remained so winsomely obvious that countless people in cities over North America, in hospitals, in churches, in small groups, on retreats and at conferences, have been encouraged to place their full trust in Christ. Bob makes Christ's presence real to those he meets. He makes up what is lacking in Christ's afflictions, for the sake of his body.

Paul's Love and Praise for Colossians

The early verses of the second chapter of Colossians continue the theme of Paul's profound love and concern for these believers, and ends with Paul's high praise and his joy that these believers have a settled faith.

> *1 I want you to know how hard I am contending for you and for those at Laodicea, and for all who have not met me personally. 2 My goal is that they may be encouraged in heart and united in love, so that they may have the full riches of complete understanding, in order that they may know the mystery of God, namely, Christ, 3 in whom are hidden all the treasures of wisdom*

and knowledge. 4 I tell you this so that no one may deceive you by fine-sounding arguments. 5 For though I am absent from you in body, I am present with you in spirit and delight to see how disciplined you are and how firm your faith in Christ is. (Colossians 2:1-5)

Paul speaks once again in Colossians 2:1-5 about his struggles for these believers, and then in verse 5 he rejoices to see their good order and their firm faith in Christ. Regardless of the time, effort, weariness, inconvenience and cost, the generator of the greatest joy in the world for every Christian parent of a small child, for every parent of an adult child, for every spouse with a broken heart for a mate who doesn't know Christ, for every sensitive Sunday School teacher, for every motivated children's group leader, for every earnest pastor, for every dedicated evangelist, for every purposeful good neighbour, is to see another person come to faith and then to grow and to become a convinced and faithful child of God.

In verse 2 it is clear that Paul's pastoral concern was for all of the Christians of the Lycus River valley because he mentions the Laodiceans as well as these Colossians. Later in the fourth chapter and verse 16 he asks the Colossians to pass this letter on the Laodicean church when they themselves have finished reading it. Many or most of these to whom he writes had never met him or seen him so it's impressive that he had this deep concern for them and that they would respect him enough to read the letter and to positively respond.

Two Concerns

Paul has two concerns for them, **first** that their hearts will be encouraged and that they will be knit together in love. What's in back of this is Paul's desire for them to be strongly resistant against the winds of false doctrine that could divide them. He wants their mutual love to be their cement that holds them together against false teaching. The **second** concern is for them to develop a comprehensive knowledge of God's mystery, which is Christ himself. The false teachers spoke eloquently about secret knowledge and mystical wisdom to acquire a relationship with God. He is claiming that they didn't need to bother with nonsense because all the treasures of wisdom and knowledge are hidden in Christ so if they have Jesus as Saviour they have everything. This should dissuade them from having their heads turned by people who would try to delude them with clever arguments. The lesson ends in verse 5, with Paul's joyful expression of confidence not only in God, but also in the spiritual "**discipline**" and "**stability**" of those believers resident in Colossae.

That Masai man was known for his scars, not the Masai ritual scars, but the ones he bore for His Savior. After his resurrection from the dead, when Jesus wanted to be recognized, He did not point to his face and say, "Look, it's me," but rather he pointed to his scars, his hands and feet.

At the far end of history as the book of Revelation unfolds it, the apostle John, weeping because no one could open the special scroll, was told by an elder standing beside him in the heavenly crowd, '*Do not weep. Behold, the Lion of the tribe of Judah.*' John looked up, expecting to see a lion. But instead he saw a Lamb. He knew immediately who that Lamb was precisely because it was wounded. Our Jesus is known by His scars. He is worthy because of His scars. We have life because of His scars.

> *"Then I saw a Lamb, looking as if it had been slain, standing at the center of the throne ... Then I looked and heard the voice of many angels, numbering thousands upon thousands, and ten thousand times ten thousand. They encircled the throne and the living creatures and the elders. In a loud voice they were saying, "Worthy is the Lamb, who was slain, to receive power and wealth and wisdom and strength and honor and glory and praise!" Then I heard every creature in heaven and on earth and under the earth*

and on the sea, and all that is in them, saying: "To him who sits on the throne and to the Lamb be praise and honor and glory and power, for ever and ever!" (Revelation 5:6, 12-13)

Jesus is the mystery of God revealed, and you and I are the ministers of this news. Sensational. Our Lamb, slain, scarred, and worthy. To Him are praise and honor and glory and power.

Chapter Four

IT'S A CHRIST-CENTRED UNIVERSE

False Teaching Still Obscures The Revealed Mystery

Following his conversion to faith in Christ, Paul's theological persuasions reformed radically. Once stubbornly anti-Christ, as a prosecutor intent on stamping out Christianity, Paul became a transformed Spirit-filled campaigner to whom Christ was preeminent. With that passion and commitment to truth about God, Paul's concern for the Colossians is understandable. In a hostile world, the gospel and the truth about Jesus Christ could easily be misrepresented. It was possible that believers like those in the Colossian church could become confused. Therefore, in order to preserve the spiritual vigor of Colossian believers, Paul counseled them to avoid any version of Christianity that diminished Christ.

Paul did not want them to become sidetracked. He didn't want Christians chasing after spiritual ambiguities but rather focusing on Christ. Christ is the sum total of everything that can be known about God. Christ's supremacy extends to everything. With that assurance, believers can say "no" to intellectual sounding but empty-headed discussions with people who have not yet understood that this is a Christ-centred universe. In Colossians 2:1-23, Paul tells the Colossian Christians, many of whom are gentiles, that they are already insiders, that is, full-fledged members of the family of God and they do not need another initiation rite such as circumcision. That's right, circumcision. Some of Paul's language and concepts are challenging but they can be understood.

The symbolism in their water baptism exhibited that they buried their old lives and that they were now clean. They had risen to a new life with Christ and no power or defect or tyrant had a claim on them. Paul urged them to disregard anyone who pressured them to comply with new rules or meetings or activities as being essential to their spirituality. The prescriptions and disciplines that some people prescribe may sound pious and look impressive but will not deliver. Paul urges them to stick with Christ because then they will be healthy. What was true for Colossians is also true for us today. The prescription for redemption and holiness has not changed because Christ has not changed.

Some Christians develop guilty feelings or are even taught to feel guilt over an endless string of failures and miscarriages, such as not praying enough or not reading the Bible frequently enough, or watching too much television, or not donating sufficiently to church coffers, or for being overweight, or having a glass of wine with dinner. You name it; we can be made to feel guilty about so much that the cumulative outcome is to feel as though we are scarcely Christian. Any hope of being spiritual persons, godly and holy, vaporize when we experience such low spiritual self-esteem. In such instances, it would be easy to be persuaded that something significant is missing from our lives and that we need something more, some further experience.

Paul begins by telling the Colossian church that he is pleased with them. Paul is presently far away from these Colossian believers and although they have never met him personally, he wants them to know that they are not alone but rather he is with them in spirit.

> *"I want you to know how hard I am contending for you and for those at Laodicea, and for all who have not met me personally. 2 My goal is that they may be encouraged in heart and united in love, so that they may have the full riches of complete understanding, in order that they may know the mystery of God,*

> namely, Christ, 3 in whom are hidden all the treasures of wisdom and knowledge. 4 I tell you this so that no one may deceive you by fine-sounding arguments. 5 For though I am absent from you in body, I am present with you in spirit and delight to see how disciplined you are and how firm your faith in Christ is."
> (Colossian 2:1-5)

You Can Be Absolutely Sure About God.

Epaphras, the Colossian church founder and teacher, told Paul that in Colossae many people had become Christians but they were now being exposed to snatches of some whacko religious teachings. Paul cannot be with these Colossian Christians and they know that. Even though he is imprisoned in the city of Rome, he wants them to know that he is knit to them in spirit, as verse 5 records. "*I am present with you in spirit …*"

Paul expresses his sincere interest in the spiritual wellbeing of everyone who is living within the area of the Lycus River valley and of course that includes the tri-cities of Colossae, Laodicea and Hieropolis. He even specifically mentions Laodicea here in verse 1. In fact he asks the Colossians to share this Colossian letter with Laodicean believers. "After this letter has been read to you, see that it is also read in the church of the Laodiceans and that you in turn read the letter from Laodicea." (4:16). Laodicea was only eleven miles northeast of Colossae.

Paul has a protective purpose in mind as he writes to the Colossians. Paul wants Colossian believers to be educated fully about the person of Jesus Christ so that they understand God. He knows that the divergent arguments that may confuse or delude them will be expressed so persuasively that they will sound credible, plausible, and believable. The possibility exists that they could be deceived. The best defense that the Colossians can mount against such disruptive nonsense teaching will be if they are united by love for one another and also if they grow together in their knowledge of the mystery concerning God. He wants to encourage them with a developing knowledge of Jesus. Jesus Christ is the key to understanding all of the treasures of wisdom and knowledge. *"My goal is that they may be encouraged in heart and united in love, so that they may have the full riches of complete understanding, in order that they may know the mystery of God, namely, Christ, in whom are hidden all the treasures of wisdom and knowledge."* (Colossians 2:2,3)

God's full story is a 'mystery,' because to the world, God is concealed and unknown. Four times in this book Paul used the Greek term 'musterion,' which can be translated as 'mystery.' It was a popular word used commonly among pagan mystery religions to refer to secret information available only to exclusive groups of people. It was believed that such secret knowledge was the means of salvation but in fact, it was bogus and heretical. Whenever Paul used the word 'musterion' he used modifiers like 'disclosed' and 'made known' and 'make plain' and 'revelation.' The mystery of God is not a secret any longer. It has been disclosed and made plain and clear. God has revealed himself. Paul's argument is that in the person of Jesus, God did reveal an ancient mystery concerning himself. There are no more secrets with God. God unveiled the mystery when divine Jesus became human and lived here on the soil of this same planet that we occupy today. If you know Christ personally by believing in him, you have no need for any purported deeper wisdom or hidden wisdom. Paul said in verse 3 that all the treasures of wisdom and knowledge are in Christ. By trusting in him we are qualified to one day occupy that eternal residence that Jesus calls home. We don't need to know precisely where and what heaven is, as long as we know that Jesus will be there. All the resources of knowledge and wisdom are in him. Believe in the Son of God and you receive eternal life.

In the first chapter of the book of the Acts of the Apostles, the author Luke says that following Jesus' resurrection from death, Jesus spent the next forty days appearing to his disciples and followers, convincing them that it was truly him who was present with them. He was not an illusion. Jesus was alive. He was real. Jesus' promises were true. Jesus told his disciples to stay together in Jerusalem for the next few days after which the Holy Spirit would come upon them and empower them to be eyewitnesses everywhere in the world. The Holy Spirit would baptize them supernaturally. Having said that, right there before their eyes, Jesus was taken up bodily into the sky and enveloped by a cloud that eventually concealed him. Momentarily, above the observers' heads, two heavenly creatures appeared, looking very much like men. *"Men of Galilee," they said, "why do you stand here looking into the sky? This same Jesus, who has been taken from you into heaven, will come back in the same way you have seen him go into heaven."* Acts 1:11

Even though Philip had watched Jesus perform miracles that could not be explained logically and scientifically, Philip typified many of us with his hesitation, his reluctance, when he said this to Jesus.

> *"Lord, show us the Father and that will be enough for us." to which Jesus said, 9 "Don't you know me, Philip, even after I have been among you such a long time? Anyone who has seen me has seen the Father. How can you say, 'Show us the Father'? 10 Don't you believe that I am in the Father, and that the Father is in me? The words I say to you I do not speak on my own authority. Rather, it is the Father, living in me, who is doing his work. 11 Believe me when I say that I am in the Father and the Father is in me; or at least believe on the evidence of the works themselves." (John 14:8-11)*

After Jesus rose from the grave and made his appearances to the disciples, Thomas, with his own unsteady faith, was given permission to touch the bodily wounds of Jesus, and when he did, he fell to the floor and emotionally exclaimed, "My Lord and my God." (John 20:28)

Yes Jesus is God.

Be Satisfied To Trust Jesus

In the years that immediately followed Christ's death, Mathew, Mark, Luke and John wrote their accounts of Christ's life and teaching. Each of them made statements that referred to the divine character of Jesus. They said a virgin mother through the agency of the Holy Spirit had divinely conceived and birthed him. They said Jesus was the incarnation of the Word or logos, and that he was the creator of the earth who took on human flesh and lived among humanity. They spoke of his resurrection and his return to earth. They spoke of the promise of forgiveness of sin and of people becoming new creations and of being filled with God's Spirit and being granted eternal life, all based upon trusting in Jesus. This is the faith that apostles taught and which Paul endorses and teaches to the Colossians and everyone else.

Paul gives an earnest appeal to the Colossian Christians.

> 6 "So then, just as you received Christ Jesus as Lord, continue to live your lives in him, 7 rooted and built up in him, strengthened in the faith as you were taught, and overflowing with thankfulness." (Colossians 2:6,7)

This is healthy advice for living the Christian life. Of course, you can use your intellect. You can develop an investigative mind. You can question things. You can be discerning, yet Paul would urge that inquiry and investigation be rooted in apostolic teaching. How did your Christian life begin? God was gracious to you, perhaps brought someone to you who told you about Jesus, or maybe you were invited to an event where the gospel was taught, or you read a book or watched a television show where the spiritual lights went on for you and you put your trust in Jesus to save you from punishment for your sins and to give you a new life, a fresh beginning. It was something like that wasn't it?

You began your Christian life by faith. You received Christ by faith. Then Paul pursues this further. Why would any of us think for a moment that moving on from that early faith, God would require anything different, anything other than faith? Why would we entertain the notion that our new lives should revert to performance and to proving ourselves? Walk the walk in the same way as you started it, that is, by faith. So in verse 7 Paul uses a metaphoric idea for this continuing lifestyle, that of being rooted like a seed germinating and taking root and spreading its roots widely so it takes in all the nutrients of sound teaching and then like a plant, we build and grow and become established and we overflow with thanksgiving to God.

In verse 6 Paul says, *"So then, just as you received Christ Jesus as Lord, continue to live your lives in him."* Continue to live in him, or in relationship with him by faith and develop that faith by learning. Become stronger, more convinced, more certain, more confident in your knowledge about God. The use of our time is an important consideration for a developing Christian. We live in an e-age, and unless we exercise control, we may easily be obsessed with electronic devices, videos, games, texting, social networking and googling. The conveniences of our modern technologies can consume us and leave little time for pursuit of God. It could be a concern that churchgoers are reading novels more frequently than they are reading the bible, browsing more internet sites and watching television more than they are spending time talking to God. The maxim is, 'by faith everything.' That being the case, wake to a new day by faith. Plan the day, make the call, have that conversation, make that visit, settle that conflict by faith. Do it all by faith. Apologize, read for pleasure, make that purchase, and resist that temptation by faith. Everything should be by faith. As you received Christ Jesus as Lord, continue to live your lives in him.

When listening to prominently visible and well-published communicators who say things that compete with long held views and doctrines, we need to be well taught, informed, discerning and vigilant. Joseph Prince is a 40 year old captivating, fiery and confident megastar televangelist, senior pastor of New Creation Church in Singapore, one of Asia's biggest churches and already on North American television. He has said, "I thank God for my roots in the Word of Faith teachings. It is truly on the shoulders of great men of God like Brother Kenneth E. Hagin that we are able to see further into the Word of God today. Brother Hagin truly had a special revelation of faith from the Lord."

Hagin has sometimes been called the father of the Word of Faith movement. Preachers within this tradition maintain that if Christians are not healthy and wealthy it is because of their lack of faith or knowledge. That opinion conveys that Christians have control over their lives by the words that they speak. Therefore, if they speak sickness and poverty they will be sick and broke. Conversely, if Christians speak blessings and healing, they will be healthy and have wealth. Nothing but blessings are intended for believers. Wealth is intended for all Christians. That's the way 'Word of Faith' thinking moves. In his book 'A Different Gospel,' D.L. McConnell reported that Kenneth Hagin said that God not only wants to deliver believers from poverty, "He [also] wants His children to eat the best; He wants them to wear the best clothing; He wants them to drive the best cars; and He wants them to have the best of everything," (p.175). To that I say, sorry, but that is baloney.

Avoid Religious Baloney

In Verse 8 Paul is cautioning believers. Perhaps, his choice of words such as, 'philosophy' and 'empty deceit' and 'human tradition' and 'elemental spirits of the world', make it difficult for us to grasp the nature of the exact threats that existed in Colossae, against which Paul is making this warning. Principally, Paul was alerting Christians against religious sounding, but false, worldly, even crude spiritual forces.

> *8 "See to it that no one takes you captive through hollow and deceptive philosophy, which depends on human tradition and the elemental spiritual forces of this world rather than on Christ." (Colossians 2:8)*

We street-proof children with warnings to pay no attention to strangers and to move away from them as quickly as possible. That's the idea behind Paul's urging of Colossians not to be duped by unscrupulous people, not to be led away captive like a prize won by charming you with high-sounding nonsense. Do not listen or believe anything you are told that does not match what you know about Christ, or that diminishes Christ's Lordship over you, or that directs your attention toward some other loyalty or priority or value other than Jesus.

Colossae was a predominantly Gentile community, principally populated by Greeks, plus a lesser percentage of Jews and others. Paul used the Greek language for this letter. The Greek word for wisdom was σόφια (sophia) and a sophos was a wise person. A sophist was an intellectual reputed to have wisdom. Sophists were philosopher-teachers who traveled in Greece teaching their students everything that was necessary to be successful in life and commonly sophists were skeptics, agnostic or atheists. Gradually sophists charged money for service and eventually sophists were portrayed as deceptive phonies. Some people are able to make false arguments appear as true statements and that is sophistry, fallacious arguments employed for the purpose of deception. We still use the term "sophisticated" to refer to intelligent or crafty people. Paul is concerned about teachers who were able to present plausible but mistaken and even misleading arguments, reasoning from traditions or basic elements of the world. This apprehension primarily related to Gnostic heresies. Comedian Steve Martin starred in a movie called 'Leap of Faith,' a spoof on faith healers in which a promotional display advertises his faith healing service with the slogan, 'Real Miracles – Sensibly Priced." It could really be humorous if it were not so accurate.

At the age of 27 I began pastoring in a small Ontario, Canada town with a population of 10,000 people. The town was home to several denominational churches, Presbyterian, Anglican, United, Pentecostal, Baptist and the Associated Gospel Church that I pastored. My youthful enthusiasm was inexhaustible with a constant flow of ideas as well as the energy to make the ideas come to life. Thinking that the local newspaper should have an evangelical news column I convinced the editor to let me write. After reading one of my sample pieces, he gave me the unheard of opportunity to write a weekly article with no limit on length. At the time, American faith healer Kathryn Kuhlman, with her long hair and ankle length dresses fluttering beatifically, was pushing miracle seekers on the forehead and saying, "take all you need." They fell backward (under the power) into the waiting arms of her crew of catchers. Her base location was a church in Pittsburgh PA. Her reach was far beyond that, even to our small town far to the north. Her twice-daily radio program and her regular TV shows enjoyed an incredibly wide audience. Each week from our Eastern Ontario town, charter buses filled with people eager for healing, travelled to Pittsburgh. Someone offered to pay my way and I accepted, thinking that I needed to understand this phenomenon and believing that it could inform my newspaper writing. I returned to my home church convinced that God would rather have me lead my congregation to believe him for healing and miracles by speaking with him directly, rather than relying upon an intermediary. Another Ontario pastor named Benny Hinn, ten years younger than me, lived in Toronto and at the age of 21 he also attended a Kuhlman service. Unlike me, Hinn came home with a resolve to become a faith healer using some of the same techniques Kuhlman used. He has succeeded in gaining celebrity status with a worldwide audience, some bizarre theological ideas, such as God is a trinity and each person within the trinity is also a trinity, so there are nine persons in God (program on TN, 10/20/90). His organization gave gifts to Tsunami relief and New Orleans flood disaster relief and other similar needs to the tune of a few hundred thousand dollars each, yet his organization receives a reported $100 million per year in donations from people yearning to receive something far greater than what they already have in Christ.

During the past sixty years North American history is sated with personalities like Hinn, Oral Roberts, Peter Popoff, Jim Bakker, Jim Jones, Todd Bentley, Maurice Carullo, Paula White, Jack Hayford, Joyce Meyer, TD Jakes, Jimmy Swaggart, Reihnhard Bonnke, John Hagee, Joel Osteen, Kenneth Copeland, Crefler Dollar Jr., everyone of whom has built a small affluent empire, exhibiting conspicuous consumption. Copeland has reportedly been able to brag that he is a billionaire because that was God's assignment for him. Whether or not those people whom I have mentioned qualify for censure is yours to decide, but I am suggesting that what Paul was saying to Colossians, about not being led away and led astray by charlatans, applies here. It's easy to become swayed by personality and zing and lose sight of the Saviour who deserves entire allegiance.

If spiritual distractions don't come from Christian counselors as I have alluded, there is an inundation of other spiritual formation advisors today who are ready to pump their muddled new age philosophies, people like Wayne Dyer, Eckhard Tolle, Deepak Chopra.

If You Have Christ, You Understand Deity

> *"9 For in Christ all the fullness of the Deity lives in bodily form, 10 and in Christ you have been brought to fullness. He is the head over every power and authority. 11 In him you were also circumcised with a circumcision not performed by human hands. Your whole self ruled by the flesh was put off when you were circumcised by Christ, 12 having been buried with him in baptism, in which you were also raised with him through your faith in the working of God, who raised him from the dead." (Colossians 2:9-12)*

Genesis tells us that humanity, both genders, male and female was created in God's image, underscoring that the likeness to God was not physical but rather spiritual and moral. When God was about to create the first human, he said, "let us make man in our image." Adam and Eve were not gods, and were not created to be gods. They were however, to be reflections of God in a human form. Much later the second person of the trinity, Christ, who was already God before his incarnation, was born to his earthly mother Mary, grew into adulthood and demonstrated to humankind what humanity in God's image should be and can be in human flesh. With this in mind, Paul reminds the Colossians and us as well in Colossians 1:15 that, *"The Son is the image of the invisible God ...."* He is not godlike. He is actually God. When he lived on earth, he was God in a human body. All who believe this and who trust in him, become new creations, but they do not become gods. Rather they are human children of God, humans who now have a heavenly Father. To make sure that we understand this distinction between humans and Jesus Christ, Paul said in 1:19, *"For God was pleased to have all his fullness dwell in him (Jesus)."* Here in Colossians 2:9 Paul chose to be even more precise and used the word "theotes" which means "deity." *"For in Christ all the fullness of the Deity lives in bodily form..."*

Paul tells the Colossians that if you have embraced Jesus by faith, then you have in him everything there is to know about God until we are at last in his presence. He fills you. Paul writes, *"...and in Christ you have been brought to fullness"* (verse 10). You are absolutely complete with Christ, and entirely secure in him because over every imaginable power source or authority, Jesus is supreme head.

Gnostics maintained that if you wanted to believe in Jesus that was fine, but you needed to add to that, other religious experiences and practices. Paul counters with what sounds like perplexing dialogue, the use of the term, 'circumcision' (verse11). While the word seems awkwardly placed, it should not be avoided, not if we truly desire to understand the scripture. It's a curious analogy, even a little discomforting that Paul links circumcision to his definition of spirituality and godliness, yet it is rooted in the Old Testament. We must understand Paul's use of the term 'circumcision.' Today male infant circumcision is a simple and virtually painless procedure of removing the foreskin sheath of the penis. The decision to circumcise the male infant can be based upon personal, religious or cultural factors. Some research demonstrates medical benefits among which are reduction of infections, sexually transmitted diseases and cancer. For adult males, circumcision is a more difficult and uncomfortable procedure. God commanded Abraham and the men of Israel that circumcision should be recognized as the sign of a new identity and the new covenant between God and the human. Therefore every male had to be circumcised (Genesis 17). As a covenantal sign it meant the men were clean and holy. Uncircumcised people were considered unclean. Such was the intent of the imagery. That was Old Testament.

But what if a Jew overvalued circumcision and relied upon his having been circumcised but he proceeded to break other commandments? It was in Romans 2 that Paul demonstrated that he was beginning to reinterpret circumcision as a spiritual concept.

> *25 "Circumcision has value if you observe the law, but if you break the law, you have become as though you had not been circumcised. 26 So then, if those who are not circumcised keep the law's requirements, will they not be regarded as though they were circumcised? 27 The one who is not circumcised physically and yet obeys the law will condemn you who, even though you have the written code and circumcision, are a lawbreaker. 28 A person is not a Jew who is one only outwardly, nor is circumcision merely outward and physical. 29 No, a person is a Jew who is one inwardly; and circumcision is circumcision of the heart, by the Spirit, not by the written code. Such a person's praise is not from other people, but from God." (Romans 2:25-29)*

Here in Colossians, Paul's argument is that circumcision is unnecessary for membership in a divine covenant relationship with God. That persuasion is instrumental in separating Christianity from Judaism. In fact in Colossians 2:12 Paul completely changes the understanding of circumcision and uses it rather as a metaphor, as a term to illustrate something else. He speaks of a circumcision affected without human hands. It's not cutting off flesh but rather cutting off nature, the natural wicked human nature. By trusting in Jesus Christ, Paul says the Colossians were circumcised by Christ, and clearly he is referring not to a physical circumcision but to some kind of non literal but nonetheless actual cutting off of their sinful nature. All people have sinned and we fall short of God's glory because we are unholy and unclean and we need clean hearts, so Christ affects a spiritual cleansing of the heart, the putting off of the body of sins and discarding of sins, a kind of genderless or gender-free circumcision so that every man, woman, boy and girl who trusts in Jesus, becomes a member of the family of God.

Then, Paul mixes metaphors by referring to burial and baptism and that could be confusing unless we understand the symbolism being referenced here which is a far more relevant symbol of the covenant relationship that all believers are able to have with God. I am a Christian. I am a child of God. I am a disciple. I am a follower of Jesus. I'm not happy calling my allegiance to Jesus, a religion, although I know that clerically it must be classified as a religion. Social scientists want to view religion as a cultural system or an anthropological category and many religions have narratives, symbols, traditions and sacred histories that give meaning to life or to explain the origin of life and of the universe. Christianity corresponds on all those points but my objection to calling my personal faith in Christ a religion is my conviction that I am involved in a relationship rather than a religion. Mine is not merely a belief system. My relationship with Christ is not just the same as the other 4200 religions of the world.

Gentile Christians in Colossae knew nothing about Old Testament laws and practices. They knew nothing about circumcision because it had not been commanded to them as with Jews, as a sign of their covenant with God. Gentiles had simply believed and then they had been baptized. Paul seeks to make readers apprehend that everything they need and all that they want to be spiritually has already been done. They don't need to strive for anything more, specially not what false teachers seek to foist on them. If death is the penalty for sin, then Jesus died as a substitute for them and since he was buried, they have been effectively buried too. Jesus did not stay dead and therefore believers possess all the hope and future and promise that the risen Christ at the right hand of the Father can imply. We don't need more.

This is reiterated in so many words in verses 13 & 14, when Paul writes that each of us had an archived leger of sins which was nailed to the cross when he was hung there, so that's all out of the way now and he has forgiven our sins and we are alive with him.

> *13 "When you were dead in your sins and in the uncircumcision of your flesh, God made you alive with Christ. He forgave us all our sins, 14 having canceled the charge of our legal indebtedness, which stood against us and condemned us; he has taken it away, nailing it to the cross. 15 And having disarmed the powers and authorities, he made a public spectacle of them, triumphing over them by the cross." (Colossians 2:13-15)*

Paul's proposition is that faith in Christ plus nothing more equals forgiveness & redemption & wholeness and he has developed this in verses 11-15.

Then in verse 15 Paul mentions rulers and authorities. What troubled people need most is a right relationship with God. Everything else is a placebo. We have developed in our culture a therapist mecca. Messed up pastors become life coaches. Dr. Phil types proliferate the television channels. People bring their problems and the human spirit is being treated with occultic, Buddhist inspired, new age, quasi-religious notions for self-fulfillment. Even Christians bring their problems to therapists looking for psychological answers for spiritual issues. Furthermore, a lot of preaching sounds like a shrink's attempt to provide serenity rather than the gospel of forgiven of sins and reconciliation with God. Our growing reliance on therapy reflects our failure to depend entirely on Christ. How did you start with Christ? Well then, continue that way, believing him. He is the answer to spiritual contentment,

To the extent that Christian worship and witness are determined by something or someone other than Christ, they will fail to produce a congregation that participates with Christ in God's salvation. Now Paul gives a couple of commands. He means them. The first one is in verse 16-17 and the next is in verse 18.

Don't Tolerate Groundless Judgement

> *16 "Therefore do not let anyone judge you by what you eat or drink, or with regard to a religious festival, a New Moon celebration or a Sabbath day. 17 These are a shadow of the things that were to come; the reality, however, is found in Christ." (Colossians 2:16-17)*

Paul was urging believers not to be intimidated by others who have made themselves spiritual umpires. These people watch to see whether the community is observing the holy days and the dietary regulations because it has been assumed that compliance means spiritual fitness. Don't put up with anyone pressuring you in details of diet, worship services, or holy days. All those things are mere shadows cast before what was to come; the substance is Christ.

This is nothing new. Christians everywhere have always been struggling with similar questions about what constitutes holy living. Here was the problem as Paul saw it. Annual religious festivals, a New Moon celebration, a Sabbath Day, monthly meetings and weekly observances had been obligatory for Judaism to look forward to the Messiah's deliverance of Israel and the promise of Shalom. But Jesus has already come and when a Christian participated in such Jewish celebrations it was like denying Jesus' Messiahship. Paul urges Christians not to let people judge you and distract you from the most important social and spiritual measurement, faith in Jesus as Lord. He is not opposed to religious celebrations or even worship that borrowed from Jewish traditions because he knows they are

God in the Open

merely shadows, or impressions that point to what is real and true. Paul was not anti-Jewish, just opposed to Jewish practice as a measurement of spirituality or even a replacement of core Christian convictions.

Paul has mentioned these admonitions elsewhere and in greater detail. In Romans 14 and 15 he wrote at great length about how to treat each other, specially knowing that we come to our Christian faith from different backgrounds and with different degrees of experience and understanding. For instance, Paul spoke of some Jews who may have placed their faith in Jesus Christ as the promised Messiah and they may approach living this new Christian life with the desire to hold on to some of the requirements from Jewish law such as their dietary restrictions and keeping certain holy days and observing the Sabbath Day with its rules. Romans 14:1-17

Don't Accept People's Interference

Here was yet another philosophical issue about which Paul wanted these Colossians to be warned. Paul mentions the worship of angels. Gnosticism asserted that God was so far above humanity and humans were so out of touch with God that the only way to worship him was indirectly through the worship of angels that he had created. Gnosticism conceived of a list of spirit beings through whom God could be approached.

> *18 Do not let anyone who delights in false humility and the worship of angels disqualify you. Such a person also goes into great detail about what they have seen; they are puffed up with idle notions by their unspiritual mind. 19 They have lost connection with the head, from whom the whole body, supported and held together by its ligaments and sinews, grows as God causes it to grow. (Colossians 2:18,19)*

From The Message, Paul's same caution sounds like this.

> *"Don't tolerate people who try to run your life, ordering you to bow and scrape, insisting that you join their obsession with angels and that you seek out visions. They're a lot of hot air, that's all they are. They're completely out of touch with the source of life, Christ, who puts us together in one piece, whose very breath and blood flow through us. He is the Head and we are the body. We can grow up healthy in God only as he nourishes us." (Colossians 2:18,19)*

Fundamentalist and evangelical Christians are known for drafting creeds of right beliefs and right conduct to separate themselves from the world. Some of the lists by which you may have lived your life might include abstaining from certain foods and drinks and practices that other mainstream Christians feel are harmless. Lists tend to lead to self-righteousness and the opinion that the more you abstain, the more spiritual you are. Isn't that the way it goes? The more fastidiously you comply with rules of self-denial the greater your holiness. Well that doesn't wash with Paul. For him, the mark of true religion is not a rigorous compliance to rules of self-denial, but rather faith in Christ and a life in his Spirit. What finally defines true Christianity is "being in Christ," where God's grace transforms people into an alternative faith community. Any definition of Christianity that substitutes regulations of self-denial for self-transformation by the grace of God is spiritually impoverished and finally useless.

So, then, if with Christ you've put all that pretentious and infantile religion behind you, why do you let yourselves be bullied by it? "Don't touch this! Don't taste that! Don't go near this!" Do you think things that are here today and gone tomorrow are worth that kind of attention? Such things sound impressive if said in a deep enough voice. They even give the illusion of being pious and humble and ascetic. But they're just another way of showing off, making yourselves look important.

> **20** *Since you died with Christ to the basic principles of this world, why, as though you still belonged to it, do you submit to its rules:* **21** *"Do not handle! Do not taste! Do not touch!"?* **22** *These are all destined to perish with use, because they are based on human commands and teachings.* **23** *Such regulations indeed have an appearance of wisdom, with their self-imposed worship, their false humility and their harsh treatment of the body, but they lack any value in restraining sensual indulgence. (Colossians 2:20-23)*

Paul bluntly asks believers, why are you still submitting to rules such as don't handle, don't taste, don't touch? (Verses 20b-21)

I remember when going to the cinema and the drive-in theatre were forbidden activities among Christians. You wouldn't dare watch a Hollywood movie, or go for a meal in a restaurant that served alcoholic beverages. Pub food might have had a quality reputation but it was out of bounds. Of course I am looking back over a few decades. My wife and I were enrolled in a Christian college and on a date night we decided to go watch a theatre showing of The Sound of Music. We were disciplined for that offence. Within Christian circles with which I am familiar today, attitudes toward alcohol consumption and dancing have changed. There is far greater latitude for personal choices, beliefs and practices. Something that is not negotiable is the prohibition against prescribing your chosen behaviour as necessary for other Christians. Paul tells Christians not to let other people pass judgment on them.

A transformed life and profound spirituality starts on the inside and moves outward from there to affect conduct. It doesn't start with rules on the outside. The decision whether or not to consume alcohol or use tobacco is more complex. The Bible allows for the enjoyment of alcohol in moderation, but it also strongly warns against drunkenness and addiction, which overpowers wise and reasonable behaviour and hinders personal development. Alcohol abuse has many long-lasting negative physical, social and academic consequences. The Bible commends leaders who abstained from, or were not addicted to, alcohol. When considering the myriad of entertainment options available, including print media, television, film, music, video games, the internet, theatre, concerts, social dancing, clubs, sports, recreation, and gambling, the expectation is that God's people will make personal choices according to biblical priorities, and with careful consideration for the immediate and long-term impact on one's own well-being, the well-being of others, and the well-being of the Church. Entertainment choices should be guided by the pursuit of activities that are edifying, beneficial and constructive, and by a preference for those things that are "true, noble, right, pure, lovely, admirable, excellent, and praiseworthy," recognizing that truth and beauty appear in many differing forms, may be disguised, and may be seen in different ways by different people.

Murray was the son of a woman who attended the first church that I pastored. He was one of the people for whom our congregation prayed when I challenged our people to take God seriously and to pray to Him directly for all our needs. Several of those for whom we prayed came to know Christ within the time I was at the church. I didn't learn about Murray's conversion until many years later. About one year ago, a woman who was of college age when I knew her during those years, came to visit us. We learned that Murray had become a Christian shortly after I moved on to another church and this woman had married him. They had a happy life together and he attended church with her and was growing spiritually. He wished to be baptized and to join the church, but he was still struggling to give up smoking. The church leadership refused him baptism because he smoked. He was hurt and confused. He continued to love the Lord and to read his Bible but he never returned to church. I can only wonder, if the umpires had not been so strict and so rules-oriented, whether Murray might have remained within the church and whether eventually he would have learned how to relax the grip of nicotine to be smoke free, and in the process become a valuable contributing member of the church. Not far from where I live is a church that encourages attendees from half-way houses and detox venues. Knowing that many of these people smoke, the church has a designated outside smoking area in compliance with our provincial anti-smoking regulations. It's a clearer signal of welcome. We all have addictions and afflictions with which we deal.

I return briefly to verse 6, *"So then, just as you received Christ Jesus as Lord, continue to live your lives in him,"* and I encourage us to resolve that having begun by faith we will continue to walk by faith.

Chapter Five

NEW POWER FOR CHANGE

Your New Identity Comes With New Power For Change

Our ship sat at rest in Glacier Bay, turning gently for passengers to see enormous walls of ice that had moved progressively from mountain peaks to sea level. As impressive as this was, it could not prepare me for my flight aboard a Wings Airway Cessna 208 floatplane soaring over five glaciers that comprise the Juneau Icefield covering 1500 square miles of breathtaking blue ice cornices and crevasses. That high altitude observation gave me a superior appreciation for glaciers, their development and recession.

An elevated perspective also enables the follower of Christ to discern some things more comprehensively. In this third chapter Paul will inform the Colossians that an elevated viewpoint will enable them to recognize personal sin and to deal with it. Sin can go unnoticed or ignored in the ordinary course of living life. Paul tells the Colossians to eliminate from their lives everything that is inappropriate to Christian living. With a lofty viewpoint, the outcome will be predictably successful. If they can better see how detestable some behaviour is to God, there is an improved likelihood that they can censor it. Paul mentions some disagreeable behaviour and thought.

> *"Put to death, therefore, whatever belongs to your earthly nature: sexual immorality, impurity, lust, evil desires and greed, which is idolatry." (Colossians 3:5)*

Christians know that such conduct is alien to holy living and may even make frequent and futile attempts to renounce these behaviours. Paul does not want the Colossian to tolerate or excuse sinful activities but rather to kill them off, eliminate them. Put them to death he says in verse 5. The first four verses are the preface that makes all the difference in dealing with unhealthy behaviour. Paul urges believers to lift their eyes and hearts and minds all the way up to Christ, where he presently resides with the Father. Paul sincerely believes that when a follower of Jesus lives everyday life as though looking at it from heaven, this superior viewpoint will enhance a person's desire and ability to make changes and to improve.

> *1 "Since, then, you have been raised with Christ,* **set your hearts** *on things above, where Christ is, seated at the right hand of God. 2* **Set your minds** *on things above, not on earthly things. 3 For you died, and your life is now hidden with Christ in God. 4 When Christ, who is your life, appears, then you also will appear with him in glory." (Colossians 3:1-4)*

Cultivate A Realistic And Heavenward Attitude To Living

Into the first four verses are interwoven many theological ideas. Paul mentions both Christ's resurrection and alludes to the believer's resurrection as fundamentally tied to Christ's. "*...you have been raised with Christ*" (verse 1), and "*you life is now hidden with Christ in God*" (verse 3). Paul speaks of Christ's heavenly position at God's right hand. He also speaks of a Christian's disinclination to earth but with a disposition toward heaven. "*Set your minds on things above, not on earthly things,*" (verse 2). Paul makes the assertion that believers have died with Christ and that their true lives are now secured with Christ forever. Then, Christ's promised re-appearance is linked with the guaranteed appearance of Christians in glory with Christ. "*When Christ, who is your life, appears, then you also will appear with him in glory*" (verse 4).

There is a genuine sense in which a Christian's life has taken on a new 'out of this world' dimension. Here is Paul's reasoning. The Christian already has an implicit resurrection life based on the reasonable deduction that Jesus died our death sentences for us. Christ's resurrection convincingly revealed that the penalty was paid, and because he rose to life, so did we. He is alive and so are we. He arose, lived here briefly and then ascended rightfully to where he belongs. We effectively rose with him and we live here for a time as well but not unaided, but rather with the Spirit of God living inside us. That's a resurrection life. Here it is again. When Jesus' lifeless body stirred to life and stood up and sauntered out of the tomb, we were in him and with him. We have resurrection lives now. Paul is compelling the Colossians to think of their Christian lives like that and the Spirit of God is convincing us to do the same. This is not a mind game, a pretense. This is not madness and mystical nonsense. This is God's method for the followers of Jesus to live here and now in readiness for our translations.

The way that God looked at it, Jesus identified with your sin and my sin and the sins of the Colossians and he died not by mistake or as a victim but deliberately to atone for that sin and to justify us before God. When Jesus rose to life from the dead, he delivered to every person who believes in him, a new life, a new relationship with God, an affinity for God, cleansing, forgiveness, righteousness and spiritual attributes so we show that we are members of God's family. That is what has taken place if you have already trusted in Jesus Christ. Trusting him is the very next thing you should do if for some reason you have been holding back. Say to him, "Lord Jesus, I believe that you are the Son of God. I confess that I am a sinner and I believe that you died for me. I accept you as my Saviour and I choose to honour you as the LORD of my life."

Thumbs up or thumbs-down hand gestures commonly indicate

approval or disapproval. Without the gestures, the English terms themselves are sometimes used as metaphors. For instance, the movie critic may write, "The audience gave the movie a thumbs-up," meaning the audience approved what they saw, regardless of whether the actual gesture was made. Thumbs up aptly fits this third chapter of Colossians. The icon of a Christian life ought to be "thumbs up." It means "all is well," and it is also a reminder to Christians as to where our true resource lies. Twice in this short section the apostle urges us to set our minds and our hearts on "things above, where Christ is seated at the right hand of God." Just as the thumb points upward, even so Christians are to look to "things above" for their help in living life here and now. Here is the sequential thinking. Since you died with Christ and you rose with Christ, it is high time that you decide to live the rest of your life in the realities of heaven because that is where your real life is and where your hope and your future reside. Let heaven be real to you, to influence your way of life. "*I go to prepare a place for you,*" were Jesus' own words. John the disciple who was a personal companion of Jesus heard him and reported it.

> *"Do not let your hearts be troubled. You believe in God; believe also in me. My Father's house has many rooms; if that were not so, would I have told you that I am going there to prepare a place for you? And if I go and prepare a place for you, I will come back and take you to be with me that you also may be where I am. You know the way to the place where I am going." (John 14:1-4)*

Paul issues two directives in Colossians 3:1-2, *'set your hearts on things above'* and *'set your minds on things above.'* Your hearts should be oriented above because that's where Jesus is now. He at the right hand of God, and the right hand was the traditional place of honour. Paul was not making this up. The gospel writers' testimonies corroborated this. "*After the Lord Jesus had spoken to them, he was taken up into heaven and he sat at the right hand of God."* (Mark 16:19)

Luke narrated how Jesus was brought before the Council of chief priests and teachers of Judaic law who "said many other insulting things to him. At daybreak the council of the elders of the people, both the chief priests and the teachers of the law, met together, and Jesus was led before them. 'If you are the Messiah,' they said, 'tell us.' Jesus answered, 'If I tell you, you will not believe me, and if I asked you, you would not answer. But from now on, the Son of Man will be seated at the right hand of the mighty God.'" (Luke 22:65-69)

Jesus demonstrated an attitude to life and even to adversities that is worth repeating. He lifted his heart and eyes toward heaven. Lift your sightline; lift your vision to see beyond here. Orient your life, fix your heart and fix your mind on things that are above. Why? Because you have been raised with Christ, Paul tells the Colossian believers, and furthermore, Christ now has been elevated to the right hand of God. It was in Colossians 2:20, that Paul mentioned our connection with Christ's death. *"Since you died with Christ to the basic principles of this world, why, as though you still belonged to it, do you submit to its rules?"* Believers are identified with Christ's death from the moment that they believe that he died for them. Now in Colossians 3 Paul begins with the corollary of that earlier statement. *"Since, then, you have been raised with Christ..."* I know that most of our English Bibles express it as "If" you have been raised. However, Paul was not expressing doubt, so this should not be interpreted as uncertainty as to whether the professing Colossian believers were risen with Christ. It is exactly the opposite emphasis, so it is better rendered *"since you have been raised with Christ,"* and that's the way NIV translated it. Therefore, since you have been raised with Christ to the place of honour at God's side, don't occupy your mind with transient and low

God in the Open

level matters, and ideas, the nonsense that is beneath this new level to which you have ascended by faith.

Verse 3 reiterates that the spiritual identification of a believer with Christ in respect to both the death and resurrection of Jesus Christ is integral to Christian teaching. It marks the end of one kind of life and the beginning of something brand new. It is the difference between darkness and light, between lost and found, between despair and hope, life and death. Understanding this is the prescription for being all that we can be here and now, in anticipation of a day when we will, not just virtually, but actually appear with Jesus Christ in glory. *"When Christ, who is your life, appears, then you also will appear with him in glory."* (verse 4).

When you set your hearts on that place and on that reality, you realize that you are looking at life on earth through Christ's eyes. You determine to bring everyday living into harmony with your reality, your lofty position with Christ. You are cultivating a realistic and heavenward attitude to living, and that requires some serious action. *"Put to death, therefore, whatever belongs to your earthly nature: sexual immorality, impurity, lust, evil desires and greed, which is idolatry."* (verse 5).

Make your Lifestyle Correspond with Christ's Life in Heaven.

Concentration upon right living requires a significant change in motivation because it will demand trimming. Whatever pertains to your earthly nature has to go. You have to let it die. In fact, you actually have to destroy it, put it to death, end it.

> *5 Put to death, therefore, whatever belongs to your earthly nature: sexual immorality, impurity, lust, evil desires and greed, which is idolatry. 6 Because of these, the wrath of God is coming. 7 You used to walk in these ways, in the life you once lived. 8 But now you must rid yourselves of all such things as these: anger, rage,*

> *malice, slander, and filthy language from your lips. 9 Do not lie to each other, since you have taken off your old self with its practices 10 and have put on the new self, which is being renewed in knowledge in the image of its Creator. 11 Here there is no Greek or Jew, circumcised or uncircumcised, barbarian, Scythian, slave or free, but Christ is all, and is in all. (Colossians 3:5-11)*

What is right, and what is wrong? I think we are weary of hearing about things we should not do. Even Christians are tired of it. That fatigue can be risky. A case is being made in these verses for eliminating certain actions and thoughts from our lives because in truth, we have no other option. After all, we belong to Jesus Christ and this requires responsible choices. On this planet, there are attitudes and activities typically on display universally and persistently, sexual immorality, impurity, lust, evil desires, greed and idolatry. Paul is speaking about wrong things that are alien to God and foreign to the right hand of God where Jesus is and where our lives are truly to be found since we are identified with Jesus Christ. We need to let this foreign unfaithfulness die. This is a significant challenge to us within our times and our liberal culture where so much is becoming acceptable.

We have achieved astonishing progress in science, technology, medicine and economics. It is estimated that the sum of human knowledge is doubling annually. As an informed culture are we better off than the ignorant and illiterate masses of other cultures or previous generations? Has this exponential progress equipped our society to make better choices? Not really. We have embraced the ethic of social correctness, which gives permission to live our lives however we choose as long as "it doesn't hurt anyone else." As an outcome, what was once an aberrant subculture is becoming the norm within our judicial and educational systems.

In this era of tolerance, the intolerance that remains is that which is directed against people who argue for modesty and purity. In 2013 Trinity Western University in British Columbia, a Christian university, acquired early approval for their proposal for a Law School division, but law societies in various parts of the country generated an extreme outcry. The disfavor stems from the university's Community Statement, which among other things asks students to consent to not engage in sexual activity outside of marriage. Other law schools and Deans and regional law societies who onside with equal rights and gay marriages, are ready to take the matter to court if need be to prevent a Christian university in Canada from having a law department. It is an uphill struggle for TWU. God has moved mountains before.

Paul would soon be up on charges of some kind if he was speaking to our culture and every civil rights junkie journalist would blast him. He challenges everything that our society is presently condoning. But then so does God challenge these things. As a matter of fact, verse 6 says it is, *"Because of these, the wrath of God is coming"*. Preachers and theologians cannot evade talking about the wrath of God unless one ignores or distorts scripture. God and evil do not coexist and evil is judiciously defined. Paul reminds the Colossians that such behaviour once characterized them but they became new creations in Christ, freed from the repulsive displays of an earthly nature *"You used to walk in these ways, in the life you once lived,"* (verse 7).

The Apollo Space program changed humanity's view of human life. Humankind had never seen our home planet the way we were able to see it through camera lenses from 384,403 km or 238,857 miles away. There were several images of earth that became the most duplicated images of all time. Our magnificent planet shining like a blue marble in the sea of our galaxy of cold stars. There was a real sense in which on the way to the moon, we discovered earth because we began to think differently about our planet. The American poet Archibald MacLeish wrote, "brothers who know now they are truly brothers, riding on the Earth together." Rusty Schweikart, an Apollo astronaut aboard Apollo 9, space walked and spent many minutes looking back at our earth from which he had come. The experience triggered an epiphany for him. He thought of the insanity of humans fighting over borders that were invisible to him from up there. Thousands of people in the Middle East killing each other over an imaginary line that one cannot even see. He wished he could take into space both sides in a conflict, to see the whole earth so beautiful, and say, "'Look. Look at it from this perspective. Look at that. What's important?'"

Similarly, there is much more that can be seen from the superior vantage point of sitting with Christ above. Verses 8 and 9 cite other attitudes and conducts, which must also be on our discard list. I wish this were as easy as pressing a reject button. We are exhorted to put away conduct detrimental to harmonious and holistic communal life such as rage, anger, malice or evil intentions, slander, abusive and filthy language, and dishonesty or, acting falsely to each other (3:8-9a). Anger can be an appropriate response sometimes but this forbidden anger refers to a calculated insult, the name calling that leads to rage, violent displays or attacks against another person. Malice is a seething inner hatred that looks for an opportunity for revenge and slander is the whispered or audible truths or untruths intended to destroy a reputation. Filthy talk as you expect is crude, coarse, foul words and lying is untruth spoken for an immediate gain but with the risk of ruining trust. These used to characterize your life and describe who you were to some degree. That was the way you lived life, Paul is telling these ancient ones and the Holy Spirit is telling us.

These removals require determination and consistency. But the motivation comes from the reminder in verse 9 that we have taken off our old selves like some unattractive, disgusting and worn out clothing. Our old selves or old natures with the customary practices have not been sent to a Thrift Shop or Value Village but have been placed in the trashcan. We have put on a new self. Isn't that an endearing way of looking at this transformation. It's like putting on new designer clothes. It's a brand new self verse 10 says, a new self which is constantly undergoing upgrading that increasingly associates us with our Creator's image, likeness to Christ.

Verse 11 presents a culture-bias-shattering bit of news. *"There is no Greek or Jew, circumcised or uncircumcised, barbarian, Scythian, slave or free, but Christ is all, and is in all."* All of the differentiations and discriminations that customarily divide people from each other, vaporize when Christ is factored into the equation. When Christ is in someone's life, Christ is the dominant feature. He is what defines a person, not nationality or language, or skin colour, or religious history, or economic capability. None of those elements count when one Christian looks at another Christian. Jesus is all that matters. So, yes, by all means, make your lifestyle correspond with Christ's life in heaven.

Treat Each Other Always as God's Much Loved and Holy People.

> *12 Therefore, as God's chosen people, holy and dearly loved, clothe yourselves with compassion, kindness, humility, gentleness and patience. 13 Bear with each other and forgive whatever grievances you may have against one another. Forgive as the Lord forgave you. 14 And over all these virtues put on love, which binds them all together in perfect unity. 15 Let the peace of Christ rule in your hearts, since as members of one body you were called to peace. And be thankful. 16 Let the word of Christ dwell in you richly as you teach and admonish one another with all wisdom, and as you sing psalms, hymns and spiritual songs with gratitude in your hearts to God. 17 And whatever you do, whether in word*

> *or deed, do it all in the name of the Lord Jesus, giving thanks to God the Father through him. (Colossians 3:12-17)*

In the church if which you are a member or attendee, there are individuals whom God has graciously led to Himself and then brought together in this congregation. All of you together must take responsibility for yourselves, to clothe yourselves every day with the virtues that will make it obvious to everyone that this entire church is a chosen people, loved by God and marked by holiness of life. One can only surmise at the difference this would bring about if this instruction were taken seriously. It is heartbreaking to watch the frequent occurrence of personal disagreement and conflict bringing disruption into church community and family lives. Churches rupture and people leave and go elsewhere or do not return to church at all. If for a moment we could see the Church from Christ's elevated position, to see her as beautiful, albeit a large family full of characters and misfits. Sometimes sisters argue. Sometimes brothers fight. But despite it all, family is supposed to be the place where you stick together, even when it's hard. Specially when it's hard.

Paul addressed a lot of church conflict in his letters. Nowhere do I hear him encouraging believers to bail on one another or move on down the road to a different church where it'll be easier. Instead, his letters are encouragements and coaching these urchin communities how to do this very hard and messy thing together.

Paul is telling us here that when you trust in Christ and become that new creation, the change affects not only the inside of a person but affects the way one behaves, so he repeats the clothing metaphor. It is a bit like wearing a new costume and putting on a newly designed and exquisite, finely tailored, made to measure apparel. That new you garment is fashionable because it is constantly improving, being renewed, never becomes dated, old, grungy. Instead it progressively resembles its creator himself.

For that reason alone, the interaction you have with each other, the attitudes you display, the manner with which you engage each other from now on is to be marked by nothing less than that which resembles Jesus. You and I are supposed to be look-alikes, looking like Jesus. What we now need to be wearing is Compassion like Christ's, His Kindness, His Humility, Gentleness, Patience, Tolerance and Forgiveness, specially in view of the fact that Christ forgave you. And then as the super glue that adheres all of these Christlike traits together, put on love, because more than anything love unify us and maintain the unity. Every church rift or falling out can be attributed to people forgetting to love.

In this section, Paul no longer speaks primarily to the individual person but rather speaks to the church or concerning the church as a whole. Verse 15 contains an example of Paul referring to the "one body" comprised of these believers.

> *15 Let the peace of Christ rule in your hearts, since as members of **one body** you were called to **peace**. And be thankful. 16 Let the word of Christ dwell in you richly as you teach and admonish one another with all **wisdom**, and as you sing psalms, hymns and spiritual **songs with gratitude** in your hearts to God. 17 And whatever you do, whether in word or deed, do it all in the name of the Lord Jesus, giving thanks to God the Father through him. (Colossians 3:15-17)*

All who trust in Jesus Christ are members of the one body. The content of these three verses is formulaic for a healthy church life and someone could easily deduce a convenient and cute triad of themes represented by three P's: peace, precepts and praise, or by three T's: tranquillity, teaching and thanksgiving. The formula or recipe for church health begins with peace.

> **15** *Let the peace of Christ rule in your hearts, since as members of **one body** you were called to **peace**. And be thankful.*

The metaphor Paul has in mind is likely that of a judge in the Olympic games, who serves as an umpire, a moderator in some instances, and the person who determines to whom the victory belongs and to whom the flowers and the crown belong. We might also say that when peace rules, it acts like a football referee, poised, alert, in control, calling incompleted passes, play stoppages and resumptions, penalties, first downs and touchdowns. Paul speaks about the "peace of Christ " ruling your hearts. Christ himself moved through life circumstances with poise and composure. We should let him who is our life, rule our hearts all the time. The apostle would have no other umpire among the saints than the peace of God: and the arguments he uses follow. Since Christ has established peace in your own life, and since Christ has called you and your fellow church members to his peace, then let Christ's peace dominate all of your hearts as a congregation, as one body. Be thankful. Just do it. There is so much for which to be grateful.

> **16** *Let the word of Christ dwell in you richly as you teach and admonish one another with all wisdom, and as you sing psalms, hymns and spiritual songs with gratitude in your hearts to God.*

Paul mentions "the word of Christ" and we think immediately of scripture. Teaching and mutual admonition is to be conducted with reference to God's truth as Jesus knows it and as he conveyed it when he was here. The writers of the four gospels recorded his instruction. Each and every member of the church is under an obligation to one another to learn and to become familiar with this word so that the entire church may be involved in teaching and counselling one another. Paul's admonition is to let Christ's word live lavishly inside you so that when you spend time with one another, the result is mutually beneficial, learning from one another, being encouraged and challenged and corrected by the shared wisdom of the Word. Then Paul links the music of the church to the word of Christ. Even as we sing all genres of Christian composition, psalms, hymns and spiritual songs, the word of Christ should richly inform the composition and the vocal production. It seems there is no warrant for worship wars with such latitude of music literature. Paul says church music should be characterized by thanksgiving to God. We should be known for our spirit of gratitude about everything. When visiting a town in Ecuador, South America I noticed that people didn't smile, that is, until I met Christians in the town who looked noticeably dissimilar from the others. Christ made such a difference in their lives that it affected their outlooks and their appearances. They smiled always. Salvation is a transformational gift. When we put that gratitude to song we develop a compendium of theology in psalms, and hymns and spiritual choruses.

> *17* *And whatever you do, whether in word or deed, do it all in the name of the Lord Jesus, giving thanks to God the Father through him.*

The seventeenth verse is a superb summary statement for life. It's a comprehensive standard for living as a Christian. Whatever you do today, do it in the name of Christ, giving thanks to God while you are doing it. It's up to each of us to translate this into everyday life and imagine the collective outcome if everyone in your church determines to live this way. And imagine the inspirational example our lives will be to those coming after us.

We should consider whether the generation that is coming after us, may not be seeing in us, enough to inspire them to want to sing, "All for Jesus, all for Jesus, all my being's ransomed powers, all my thoughts and words and doings, all my days and all my hours. Let my hands perform His bidding; Let my feet run in His ways; Let mine eyes see Jesus only; Let my lips speak forth His praise. Since mine eyes were fixed on Jesus, I've lost sight of all beside - So enchained my spirit's vision, Looking at the Crucified." (Lyrics: Mary Dagworthy James (1810-1883); Music: Asa Hull (1828-1917)

Chapter Six

MOTIVATED TO PLEASE THE LORD WITH LIFE CHANGES

Colossians 3:18-4:6

Paul doesn't speak to all of the evolving issues that shape our culture, but in writing to these ancients, he makes common sense comments to dads and children, servants and masters, saying,

> *18 Wives, submit to your husbands, as is fitting in the Lord. 19 Husbands, love your wives and do not be harsh with them. 20 Children, obey your parents in everything, for this pleases the Lord. 21 Fathers, do not embitter your children, or they will become discouraged. 22 Slaves, obey your earthly masters in everything; and do it, not only when their eye is on you and to win their favor, but with sincerity of heart and reverence for the Lord. (Colossians 3: 18-22)*

Paul's letter to the church at Colossae originated some time during 1 AD. This is a first century document, a personal letter written by a Jewish Christian to other Christians in Colossae. Can Paul's truncated, blunt and authoritatively stated declarations be applicable today? Is there anything insightful here, or are these first century values and ethics irrelevant to us? He talks about slaves and I can't remember my last servant's name. In our own day of liberation, equality and parity, Paul's statements made to husbands and wives will require sincere explanation. This cannot be immaterial because it is God's word and we should be able to assume that it is germane information even for our times and our families. Paul had plausible reasons for saying what he did and fortunately, in other letters Paul did say much more about marriage and the roles and relationships of men and women within marriage.

Living where we live in history, we dare not disengage from our own societal changes, so here is the current picture. The typical North American family unit is undergoing modifications and family will never be the same as it was ten, twenty, thirty years ago. In North American culture, marriage is no longer the consecrated, permanent union it once was. The proliferation of divorce, remarriage, stepfamilies, and single parenthood has transformed the family institution. According to Statcan census data from 2011 the predominant family structure is married couples at 67.0% but that's dropping. Today, one in seven families is comprised of unmarried couples in comparison to one in seventeen only fifteen years ago. Weddings are being postponed as young adults complete graduate degrees and trade certification and establish themselves in careers. Within our cultural norms couples forego the wedding ceremony and opt to live together instead in consensual unions or common law relationships. Cohabitation was obscure and even taboo throughout the nineteenth century and until the 1970s. Between 2006 and 2011, the number of common-law couples rose to 13.9%, four times greater than the 3.1% increase for married couples. Common-law couple families account for 16.7% of families. The numbers of North American cohabiting couples have risen by 170% since 1996. Same sex couple families tripled between 2006-2011, the first five-year period in which same sex marriage was legal in Canada and these account for 12.8% of families, with one third of these same sex couples being married. Gay and lesbian couples are taking in foster care kids and adopting children. Immigration from other cultures brings an entirely new dimension to Canadian family life, with extended families under the same roof. Working, paycheque Moms are a central organizing principle of our society. Single parent families increased 8.0%

between 2006-2011. These changes have occurred in European countries as well.

Sixty-five percent of the public, and seventy-two percent of adults under the age of 30, view the ideal marriage as one in which husband and wife both work and share childcare and household duties. Just 30 years ago, less than half of the population approved of the dual-income family, and less than half of one percent of husbands knew how to operate kitchen appliances and the sponge mop. The changes to family and within family affect the way churches must choose to serve people in this rapidly morphing society.

The church is not required to accommodate to the changing mores but must at least stay informed in order to know how to connect with families, how to speak to families and to how to program for families. In light of our world and our culture, we must try to apply this scripture to our lives.

In the previous chapter, the study concluded with Colossians chapter 3, verse 17 which says, *"And whatever you do, in word or deed, do everything in the name of the Lord Jesus, giving thanks to God the Father through him."* Because the thoughts of a letter generally flow, the seventeenth verse leads naturally to the verses that now pertain to family members and how as Christians we should be treating one another. All of our relationships should be conducted in keeping with the name of the Lord. Furthermore, in verses 12-14, Paul advised the Christians that holy living required showing to one another compassion, kindness, humility, meekness, patience, tolerance, forgiveness and love. These virtues should be apparent within our relationships as family, friends, and work associates. That's doing relationships and family in the name of the Lord. I will take the liberty to deal with the least controversial areas first, and secondly when we come to advice to the wives and husbands, I will reference other scripture written by Paul, where fuller explanation is provided for these abbreviated commands.

Slaves And Masters

22 Slaves, obey your earthly masters in everything; and do it, not only when their eye is on you and to curry their favor, but with sincerity of heart and reverence for the Lord. 23 Whatever you do, work at it with all your heart, as working for the Lord, not for human masters, 24 since you know that you will receive an inheritance from the Lord as a reward. It is the Lord Christ you are serving. 25 Anyone who does wrong will be repaid for their wrongs, and there is no favoritism. ... (Colossians 3: 22-25)

1 Masters, provide your slaves with what is right and fair, because you know that you also have a Master in heaven. (Colossians 4:1)

In the Roman Empire slavery was a dominant form of labor, much as working for wages or a salary is today, but slaves and masters are not exactly equivalent to employees and employers. Most laborers today are not slaves, though they might sometimes describe themselves that way at the end of a bad or tiring day at the office or the plant. The general principles that Paul puts forward concerning slaves and masters in this letter can be applied to modern employees and employers, provided we recognize the significant differences between our situation now and theirs then. Slave-owners were in a position of absolute power over their slaves, similar in some respects to, but much more extreme than the power that employers or managers have over workers today. Slaves were the property of masters and the abolition of slavery within societies has been a hard fought combat that carried on into our recent centuries. Now employees are free men and free women, often with rights safeguarded by government law, and sometimes championed through unions of employees that add weight to bargaining power.

Paul asserts that Christians should be doing honourable work for a higher reason than duty to a master. Just as we noted in Colossians 3:17, Paul stresses again in Colossians 3:22 and I am paraphrasing, *"obey all that your masters expects of you, not simply to impress them but rather* **doing it enthusiastically as though you are doing it for the Lord."**

How can we do our work wholeheartedly, *"as working for the Lord, not for human masters "* (Col. 3:23)? That phrase carries at least two ideas: **First**, if we are Christ-followers, we represent Jesus in the workplace and our treatment of others and the diligence with which we do our work reflects on our Lord. **Second**, working for the Lord or in "Jesus' name" also implies that we live recognizing that he is our master, our boss, the one to whom we are ultimately accountable.

From that thought Paul goes on to remind us that in all our work we are really working for the Lord. And that simply means that while we have accountability on a human horizontal level, most importantly, we bring diligence to our work because we recognize that eventually God is our judge, our performance assessor. God takes all labor seriously, even if it is done under imperfect or degrading conditions. Paul would not be satisfied with a shallow treatment of this principle, like putting a Bible verse on our locker or a bumper sticker on our car or any other sign or gesture because those do not constitute a Christ-centred work life. Rather, Paul would be gratified when we approach work prayerfully asking God specifically to show us how we can show respect for supervisors, bosses, workmates, accomplish more, do it better. It's a motivational issue as we fashion our daily work objectives as if God were the owner of the company. Even our work is contained within God's kingdom and is part of his agenda.

Wives and husbands, children and parents, slaves and masters are all interdependent relationships. and each pair of associations has obligations to another, specially in Christ's body. Hard on the heels of the commands to slaves comes a directive to masters (Colossians. 4:1): *"Masters, treat your slaves justly and fairly, for you know that you also have a Master in heaven."* Paul is talking to Christian Masters, and he knows that the Roman legal system grants certain power and latitude to slave owners, but he is teaching that finally masters must answer in God's courtroom where justice for everyone is upheld. There is mutual obligation under God for employers and employees to treat each other justly and fairly. A 'just wage' and 'fair working conditions' are the master's responsibility. God is watching. You have a master in heaven.

Children and Fathers

> *20 Children, obey your parents in everything, for this pleases the Lord. 21 Fathers, do not embitter your children, or they will become discouraged. (Colossians 3:20,21)*

Obedience to parents is the advice given here and the motivating reason is that this pleases the LORD. The only children that care a hoot about that are Christian children who are old enough to understand the compelling value of satisfying God's expectations of them. Among the Ten Commandments the fifth one says, *"Honor your father and your mother, that your days may be long in the land that the Lord your God is giving you"* (Exodus 20:12). The apostle Paul refers to that command when he is writing to the Christians at the church in Ephesus.

> *1 "Children, obey your parents in the Lord, for this is right.*
> *2 "Honor your father and mother" (this is the first commandment with a promise), 3 "that it may go well with you and that you may*

> *live long in the land." 4 Fathers, do not provoke your children to anger, but bring them up in the discipline and instruction of the Lord. " (Ephesians 6:1-4)*

I was in a local mall one day and heard the sound before I saw the child out of control. He was approximately four years old and was old enough to obey, but at the top of his lungs he was letting mommy know that he did not want to go where she was going and that he was not going to let up his demonstration until she relented. I might have credited her with possessing calm composure but it was clear that she was incapable of turning this thing around. It would run its course and in all likelihood he would win and even be rewarded with a hot chocolate later. I just couldn't wait long enough to watch the outcome. This observation dramatized for me the importance of coaching children early in their lives that they must obey mom and dad because it is the right thing to do because that makes God pleased with you.

I am certain that you too have also seen parents act as though they are helpless when seeking to manage a small child's behaviour. That is illogical. God will not require children's obedience to parents if it is an impossible response. Requiring obedience from children is possible. Small fry can be shown what must not be bitten or touched or spat or screamed. Requiring obedience must be started at home and consistently expected within the home on seemingly minor things and then one can reasonably expect this same obedience in the mall. If a child is out of control in public, it is certain that at home they are in control. If that is not the case, then obedience anywhere becomes optional. I have met some winsomely wonderful children, which informs me that there is consistency in their homes.

Of course this demands much effort but don't you agree that it is worthwhile? To expect obedience calls for energy. If Christian parents have themselves come from dysfunctional homes of passivity and anger, there can be a tendency to reduce anger and accentuate passivity and that's the wrong way to go. There are occasions when it may feel easier simply to let children have their way. But that is shortsighted. Uncontrollable children are no fun. They have learned what buttons to press. They have read that mommy is powerless and dad is a wimp and can be wrapped around a finger. Kids read parents. They never pull the same stunt with strangers because they haven't figured them out yet. They learn to defy just short of parental eruption. It really takes work to be instantly consistent with every disobedience.

It's curious for us that mothers are unmentioned in relationship to their children but only the fathers are cited with responsibility. It's not a serious question because in first century Colossae it was a given that mothers were vitally involved in the children's lives. They didn't need to be commanded to love their children. Among the list of credits for the classic woman of honour in Proverbs 31 are these remarks, *"she rises while it is yet night and provides food for her household…" "She is not afraid of snow for her household, for all her household are clothed in scarlet." "She looks well to the ways of her household and does not eat the bread of idleness. Her children rise up and call her blessed."* Fathers are mentioned in Colossians because it was most predictable for them to be harsh with their children. Let me simply say that both parents, mother and father are viewed as having responsibility when it comes to nurturing an obedient spirit in a child.

Paul speaks about harsh treatment of children by a father who is overbearing and severe. Do not embitter your children lest you discourage them, is the advice that Paul gives in this letter. I was in a room with a mother and father and their five children, three boys and two girls all under the age of 13. We were all there waiting for an appointment, and this family arrived prepared. Each member of the family pulled out an iPad or a MacBook Air and spent the next 90 minutes in solitary engagement with their individual screens. The only time the dad looked up from his pad was to scold the children for something they were doing whether it was tapping feet or laughing too loudly. He impressed me as either a disinterested dad or a badgering dad. If they didn't have an apple device would each child be obedient. Good fathering requires more than supplying your children with substitute child-minding devices. Sincere interest and time spent in a common pursuit reveals a good father and insures a child will have genuine incentive to obey. The onus cannot only be on children, surely. If parents slack off and fail to instruct their children to obey God's appointed authorities, those kids are being prepared for a life that is out of step with God and His word. For parents to neglect reinforcing obedience is puzzling. Christian parents must not fail to require and to receive obedience from their children. Requiring obedience of children is implicit in the scripture. God cannot possibly require children to obey parents and not require parents to expect and to receive that obedience. There is something implicit in the parent's job, the dad's job, to teach children the satisfaction of a submissive spirit. Doesn't it seem appropriate to regard parents as representing God to small children? Obedience will please the parents and that pleases God.

Wives And Husbands

> *18 Wives, submit to your husbands, as is fitting in the Lord. 19 Husbands, love your wives and do not be harsh with them. (Colossians 3:18,19)*

Within Christian circles there is significant disagreement over the words "submit" and "head." Entire movements or theological camps have developed in order to research and to defend opposing interpretative positions. Egalitarians interpret a passage such as this in a gender equal manner whereas traditionalists view it in a hierarchical manner. What was Paul thinking as he wrote? What is God saying through this inspired text? We are fortunate that Paul more fully elaborates his consistent themes in his letter to the Ephesians. Colossians does not say enough to satisfy the debate inherent within the instructions given in Colossians 3:18,19. Ephesians sheds revealing light on the abridged remarks in Colossians. It is sensible to see what else the apostle said about this subject.

As an illustration of how Ephesians benefits us, we compare Colossians 2:6 and Ephesians 5:1-2. In Colossians 2:6 Paul advises believers about on how to live life and he writes, *"As you received Christ Jesus the Lord, so walk in him ..."* They received Christ Jesus by faith, and by faith they should now continue to walk or live. That's fine, but a keen disciple appreciates further instruction and that is provided in Ephesians. In Ephesians 5:1-2 Paul explains what is meant by living life or walking in Christ, by exhorting his readers, *"Be imitators of God, therefore, as dearly loved children and **live a life of love**, just as Christ loved us and gave himself up for us as **a fragrant offering and sacrifice** to God."* Further in Ephesians 5:15-16 Paul wrote, *"Be very careful, then, how you live--not as unwise but as wise, making the most of every opportunity, because the days are evil."* Therefore, walking in him involves a life of love and sacrifice and wise actions that make the best possible use of our time.

Similarly, with regard to the marital relationship, we find that Paul's quick remark about husbands and wives in Colossians 3:18,19, receives amplification in Ephesians 5:17-33, and since we want to understand God's expectations of partners in marriage, we will look here.

17 Therefore do not be foolish, but understand what the Lord's will is. 18 Do not get drunk on wine, which leads to debauchery. Instead, be filled with the Spirit. 19 Speak to one another with psalms, hymns and spiritual songs. Sing and make music in your heart to the Lord, 20 always giving thanks to God the Father for everything, in the name of our Lord Jesus Christ. 21 Submit to one another out of reverence for Christ. 22 Wives, submit to your husbands as to the Lord. 23 For the husband is the head of the wife as Christ is the head of the church, his body, of which he is the Savior. 24 Now as the church submits to Christ, so also wives should submit to their husbands in everything. 25 Husbands, love your wives, just as Christ loved the church and gave himself up for her 26 to make her holy, cleansing her by the washing with water through the word, 27 and to present her to himself as a radiant church, without stain or wrinkle or any other blemish, but holy and blameless. 28 In this same way, husbands ought to love their wives as their own bodies. He who loves his wife loves himself. 29 After all, no one ever hated his own body, but he feeds and cares for it, just as Christ does the church-- 30 for we are members of his body. 31 "For this reason a man will leave his father and mother and be united to his wife, and the two will become one flesh." 32 This is a profound mystery--but I am talking about Christ and the church. 33 However, each one of you also must love his wife as he loves himself, and the wife must respect her husband. (Ephesians 5:22-33)

The principle of mutuality governs the entire passage of Ephesians 5:22-33. No informed person would assert that only men can be saved by grace. Since God has loved the world enough to send his own Son so that whoever believes in him will not perish but will be granted eternal life, we would enthusiastically endorse the truth that every spiritual blessing in Christ applies to both men and women. Women as well as men have been made alive with Christ? We would never teach that only men have been called to be holy and blameless? Women too, are spiritual heirs, members of the body, partakers of the promise in Christ Jesus through the Gospel? Women as well as men are urged to walk in a manner worthy of the calling to which they have been called? Women are included in the one Lord, one faith, one baptism, one God formula of inclusion into this Body, the Church? Therefore, both men and women are to grow up in every way into our head who is Jesus? Regardless of gender we are told to shed the old natures and put on new selves fashioned in the likeness of Christ? Male and female are included among those whom Paul calls *"dearly loved children"* (Ephesians 1:1). We are supposed to walk as wise people, understanding the will of God, all of us, men and women both (Ephesians 5:17).

In developing the marriage information in Ephesians 5:22-33 which informs our understanding of Colossians 3:18-20, the earlier verses of Ephesians 5:18-21 provide some essential groundwork. In verse 18 a contrast is drawn between becoming drunk by consuming too much wine and being filled with the Holy Spirit of God. *"Do not get drunk on wine, which leads to debauchery. Instead, be filled with the Spirit."* Both drunkenness and Spirit-filling speak to being controlled in mind and conduct by something outside oneself. One condition is proscribed (forbidden) and one is prescribed (directed), that is, one is prohibited and the other is preferred. One is condemned and the other is commanded. Don't be drunken! Instead, be filled with the Spirit. Both men and women may become drunk with wine. It follows that both male and female are told to be filled with God's Spirit.

The governance of the Holy Spirit or the power of the Spirit in our lives is demonstrated in at least four ways Paul says, and he names them in verses 19 and 20. Here are four participial clauses each of which modifies or completes the picture of a Spirit-filled life. In verse 19 *"addressing one another in psalms and hymns and spiritual songs"* and then *"singing and making melody to the Lord with your heart."* In verse 20, *"giving thanks always and for everything to God the Father in the name of our Lord Jesus*

Christ," and finally fourth, *"submitting to one another out of reverence for Christ."* So the command is, be filled with the Spirit and thereby demonstrate these four accompanying results in the way you live your life. In order for the last of the four results, namely, *submitting to one another out of reverence for Christ,"* to be translated into everyday relationships, Paul speaks to wives and to husbands, to children and parents and to slaves and masters. Right now we are looking exclusively at the wives and husbands counsel.

We cannot evade the straight talk of Ephesians 5:22 which says, *"wives submit to your husbands, as to the LORD,"* as does Colossians 3:18. Clearly the notion of subjection or submission by women to men appears offensive and degrading. It seems to imply the accession of an inferior person to a superior person. For sure, the text has been abused precisely in such ways within the history of the church. Without a doubt Paul's exhortation is framed during a cultural, societal setting of another time long ago. A time when the place and role of women and girls was not respected but was demeaning. And it has never surprised me that contemporary readers of these passages would look at them with unease. Is it any wonder within our culture and society that women and particularly wives react with apprehension at the sound of these words, when here in Canada, at the first federal election in 1867 women did not have the right to vote, and only privileged, British or Canadian born, mostly white women gained that right by 1917 and then all Caucasian women by 1918. Hindu, East Indian and Japanese women could not vote until the late 1940's. Aboriginal women waited until 1960 for that right. This is in Canada.

All of the understandable apprehensions that emerge from our culture which has embraced equal rights makes it imperative that we do not quickly gloss over the Ephesians 5 verse 21 participle which said "submitting to one another," which places the accent of the submission on both parties. It is a mutual submission or a mutually agreed upon submission that Paul is promoting as Holy Spirit living. I repeat, the principle of mutuality governs the entire passage. Mutual submission or surrendering to one another means 1) wives submitting to their husbands, 2) husbands loving their wives, 3) children obeying their parents, 4) fathers disciplining their children, 5) slaves serving their masters, and 6) masters caring for their slaves. These are codes of conduct and such codes were common in the cultures of that time.

The concept of mutuality between believers is a regular New Testament theme. It is the attitude that believers as members of the body should have to one another, yet early Christianity contains an unresolved tension between authority and mutuality, or as it pertains here, to mutual subordination and the authority of some. Paul is trying to help the Ephesians to think this through. Perhaps he is helping us as well.

Even though Paul does not begin in this order, I will begin with the responsibility of husbands. *"Husbands, love your wives"* (Ephesians 5:25). The Colossians 3:19 passage says, *"Husbands, love your wives and do not be harsh with them."* One might question, why Paul makes this command at all. Shouldn't it be assumed that husbands will love their wives? Why would they have married their wives at all? When Paul tells husbands to love their wives, he exceeds anything that is familiar to Graeco-Roman or Hebrew behavioural codes. What would have been expected in those societies would be words such as "husbands, rule your wives." This now became a critical Christian distinctive. When Christ redeems a man and makes him a holy and transformed servant of God, that man is expected to change. This Spiritual transformation that has changed everything for the believing male, does not merely address eternity but also temporal relationships and conduct. In marriage this ransomed man now forgoes his own comfort and safety to the point of death. This command to love his wife is an expression of the way in which the husband can also express submission for the sake of his wife.

Men, please understand that to which Paul's command commits us. To love your wife like Christ loved the church elevates this husband's love far above any emotional feeling or social convention. This is not simply a Valentine's card or a valentine sentiment. This is not a box of chocolates. It's not even a box of chocolates with a surprised diamond necklace inside. To love one's wife like this makes it impossible for a man to ever consider it appropriate to take action or to find personal fulfillment at the expense of his wife. The heart of the Gospel is the sacrifice of Christ. The substitutionary atoning death of Christ demonstrates once and for all that Christ's love for his Church was greater than his love for his own life. Of course, no one can and no one needs to repeat that saving action but we husbands illustrate the extent of Christ's love every time we love our wives like that. We must not set a lower standard for ourselves than Christ set for himself.

Some people might actually argue that the command to the men is more extreme than the command which may be deemed unreasonable to the women. It is a radical expectation because the word that Paul used to express 'love' is neither the phileo word for relational love nor the eros word for romantic love but rather agape which is a demanding form of love. Agape demands more than mere submission. If one falls out of love it was eros or something less than even that. No one can fall out of agape love. Agape is not even a felt kind of love or a sentiment. It is something that we do. It is action. Agape can therefore be commanded as Paul has commanded it here to men who have been redeemed by the blood of Christ and who are children of the Father and who are filled by the Spirit of God. Agape love is always about giving rather than getting.

Then Paul provides two measurements for this agape kind of love. In Ephesians 5:25-27 husbands are told that they must love their wives as Christ loved the church.

Then in 5:28-29 he instructs husbands to love their wives as they love their own bodies. So the two key questions for men are, How does Christ love the church? And how do men love their own bodies? The reason Paul makes such an exhortation is so that the wife may become all that God meant her to become. The church is meant to be holy and radiant as a pure bride. What a wife can become is not specified but the inference is clear that the husband must love her in such a way that her full potential in God will be realized. That's how Christ loves the Church. And as far as Spirit-filled man loving his wife as he loves his own body, he will first of all nourish his wife, see that she is fed (verses 28-29). He will give her all the nourishing attention that agape love demands or envisions.

Christian husbands have not been given special privilege but rather, special responsibility. The Church does not want to be liberated from Christ, free of him, independent of him, and the inference is that a Christian wife who is loved by a husband who loves her in a Christ-like manner, will enjoy all the liberation she wants. If husbands are fulfilling their right role toward their wives, their wives will be content with the scriptural expectation placed upon them as well.

Now, suitably and reasonably we can come back to Ephesians 5:22 and Colossians 3:18 and the instructions to wives with regard to their attitudes, viewpoints and manners of behaviour toward their husbands. I reiterate that the instruction to the husbands and now to wives was based upon the foundational expectation that being Spirit-filled, both husbands and wives would be submissive to one another each in distinct ways within the domestic and marital relationship.

What we have here is a Household Code and such codes were not uncommon in the cultures of Paul's day. The Old Testament Jews had a body of Jewish Law or precepts, which they called halakah (halacha) which pertained to moral behavioural codes and household relationships and duties. The Qumran community, from which the Dead Sea Scrolls derive, authored instruction to husbands and wives and children. There are similar codes of conduct among Stoics, Greeks and Romans. Similar codes exist in the New Testament letter of 1 Peter.

Within the societies of Paul's day, the place of the woman and the wife was not that of an equal in a relationship and was often more in line with property, goods, and assets. We must understand that in writing this, he was not merely making an accommodation to the social mores of his time but rather he was showing an awareness of a potential problem to which he was making an inspired statement. The problem was this. As women became followers of Christ and as children and slaves became Christians, their newfound freedom in Christ and equality as believers in the Body, the Church, could be viewed by critical observers as a dangerous insubordination. *"Wives, submit to your own husbands, as to the LORD."* The exemplary behaviour being recommended here and in the parallel passages in Colossians and 1 Peter aims to reduce tensions that were being created by Christianity. In Paul's day it was important that Christianity not be misunderstood by society and that new Christians not jeopardize essential unity and harmony by taking advantage of their spiritual freedom. The submission of a wife to her husband is exercised within the wider framework of mutual submission in verse 21. This is a prescription for Spirit-filled women. Submission does not mean that the wife puts her husband in the place of Christ. Rather, verse 21 said submission is proffered out of reverence for Christ. Submission is the divine expectation that the wife will honour and affirm her husband's leadership and help to carry it though according to her gifts.

"Now as the church submits to Christ, so also wives should submit to their husbands in everything," (Ephesians 5:24). When Paul describes how the church's submission to Christ is the model for the way by which wives should submit to their husbands in everything, he is not suggesting that submission accedes to a notion that the husband's word is absolute, since only Christ's word can be absolute. A wife should not follow her husband into something that is sinful. That would not be acting in reverence for Christ. Submission does not require a wife to abandon good judgement and restrict her from having input into decisions or opportunity to influence her husband. Submission does not demand that she act as if she is without knowledge, good sense and effective thinking. Submission comes rather from what is appropriate in God's created order.

The wife's submission to her husband is the inclination of her will to say yes to her husband's leadership as well as a disposition of her spirit to support his initiatives. It is both of these, an inclination and a disposition. To illustrate, I will suppose that my wife Christine hesitates at a decision that I have made. Oh it's not a stretch. It happens. My decision may look unwise to her, even foolish for us and for our family or ministry. Now if she is agreeing with Paul's instruction, she may express her submission by saying, "Ron, I know you've given this much thought and it seems right to you and I like your reasons and motivation for it but I do not think it is wise and I don't have peace about it. I think we need to talk further about it and I would like to do that after supper. Okay?" That's a reasonable expression of biblical submission because I have demonstrated before that I am fallible. Further, it should please me that Christine is keen to be involved in the decision and she can give prudent counsel. Her expression was done in such a way that she showed me she endorses my leadership and affirms my role and anticipates that our mutual submission would result in a wise decision with which both of us are content.

Since this is the marriage relationship in which both husband and wife show reverence to Christ by mutually submitting to one another in the specific ways of loving like Christ and honouring as unto Christ then let's go to the end of the chapter and the summary comment Paul makes. In verse 31 Paul quotes Genesis 2:24 and writes, "*For this reason a man will leave his father and mother and be united to his wife, and the two will become one flesh.*" In verse 32 Paul looks back on this quote and says, "*This mystery is a profound one, and I am saying that it refers to Christ and the church.*" Why is marriage a mystery? Marriage is a metaphor or a picture that stands for something far greater than the mere union of one man and one woman. It stands for the relationship between Christ and the Church. While the union between Christ and the Church are the example that marriage partners should follow, their own marriage also serves as a living illustration of Christ and the church? The deepest meaning of a marriage which is sometimes concealed but it is revealed here, is as an image of Christ and the Church, a living illustration. That is the deepest meaning of marriage.

We too often get it wrong. We assume headship and submission are the result of sin. We assume that sin invented headship and submission or sin is the explanation for it. The first three chapters of Genesis disclose that in the natural relationship between first man and first woman there was a creation ordered headship and submission but that sin ruined them. Sin ruined headship and ruined submission. Sin twisted them into behaviours against which we have angry objection. Sin twisted the husband's subservient and devoted headship into aggressive domination or lazy indifference, while at the same time twisting the woman's intelligent and agreeable submission into manipulative sweet-talking or blatant noncompliance. Sin made headship and submission ugly and revolting. So we rephrase the mandates this way. Wives, let your fallen submission be redeemed by modeling it after God's intention for the Church! Husbands, let your fallen headship be redeemed by modeling it after God's intention for Christ. Men, it is not a right to control and to dominate. It's the responsibility to love like Christ and to lay your life down for your wife in servant leadership. And women, this is not an instruction to slavishly and coercively cower in his presence. Christ is not looking for that from his Church but rather a free, willing, glad, refining and strengthening deference. This passage guards against the abuse of headship and the debasement of submission.

Headship is the divine calling of a husband to take primary responsibility for Christ-like, servant leadership, protection and provision in the home. Submission is the divine calling of a wife to honor and affirm her husband's leadership and help carry it through according to her gifts.

My father and mother have both passed away into the presence of the Lord. Mom died in November 2007 and Dad in May 2008 six months apart. They were sweethearts, married for 66 years. Our family enjoyed the way the two of them cherished one another. The evening before her funeral, when the extended family was together, we all stood by her coffin and dad broke us all by saying, "goodnight sweetheart, I'll see you soon." Six months later when dad died and we siblings went through what was left, inside his wallet was a small piece of paper, folded and faded and bearing a poem. "She was not created from his head to top him. Nor from his feet to be stepped on. She was made from his side to be equal to him. From beneath his arm to be protected by him. Near his heart to be loved by him."

Chapter Seven

A Farewell From Prison

Colossians 4:7-18

There has been little dispute that this is the apostle Paul's personal letter to the Colossian believers and since the second century AD the letter has been regarded as being God's Word. The term 'canon' derives from Greek and Hebrew words that mean 'a measuring rod' and the term canonicity describes the standard that books had to meet in order to be acknowledged as scripture. While it may seem that the selection of books to be regarded as inspired scripture is a purely human process, the vast Christian community both Catholic and Protestant have always understood that the Holy Spirit was given to the early Church to energize holy instincts so that what was genuine could be distinguished from the spurious. When Church Fathers enunciated the criteria that helped them determine which books could be accepted as canonical, they cited apostolicity, orthodoxy, catholicity, and inspiration. A letter or book had to be authored by an apostle or someone close to the apostles because that conveyed authority and credibility. Paul wrote this letter, as he himself says, verse 18, "*I, Paul, write this greeting in my own hand. Remember my chains. Grace be with you.*" The script needed to be Christocentric, that is, the person and work of Christ was principal in the writing, and it had to agree with other canonical books. The universal acceptance and application of the book in question was also a criterion. Further, the inspiration of the writing needed to be validated by the uniqueness of the message about Christ and the power that it demonstrated within the Church to purify and to change lives. The New Testament's own testimony is that "*All Scripture is God-breathed and is useful for teaching, rebuking, correcting and training in righteousness,"* 2 Timothy 3:16. The church fathers regarded the letter of Paul to the Colossians as fulfilling the criteria for inclusion among the sacred writings to comprise the New Testament. Colossians is regarded as God's Word, scripture.

I have chosen to include Paul's brief letter to Philemon in this book treatment of Colossians and my reason for doing so is contained in these concluding verses of Colossians. That reason is the mention of a man named Onesimus among a citation of several people who are important to Paul and the believers in the tri-city area. Paul finishes his encouragement to the Christians of Colossae with the following words.

> *2 Devote yourselves to prayer, being watchful and thankful. 3 And pray for us, too, that God may open a door for our message, so that we may proclaim the mystery of Christ, for which I am in chains. 4 Pray that I may proclaim it clearly, as I should. 5 Be wise in the way you act toward outsiders; make the most of every opportunity. 6 Let your conversation be always full of grace, seasoned with salt, so that you may know how to answer everyone. 7 Tychicus will tell you all the news about me. He is a dear brother, a faithful minister and fellow servant in the Lord. 8 I am sending him to you for the express purpose that you may know about our circumstances and that he may encourage your hearts. 9 He is coming with Onesimus, our faithful and dear brother, who is one of you. They will tell you everything that is happening here. 10 My fellow prisoner Aristarchus sends you his greetings, as does Mark, the cousin of Barnabas. (You have received instructions about him; if he comes to you, welcome him.) 11 Jesus, who is called Justus, also sends greetings. These are the only Jews among my fellow workers for the kingdom of God, and they have proved a comfort to me. 12 Epaphras, who is one of you and a servant of Christ Jesus, sends greetings. He is always wrestling in prayer for you, that you may stand firm in all the will of God, mature and fully assured. 13 I vouch for him that he is working hard for you and for those at Laodicea and Hierapolis. 14 Our dear friend Luke, the doctor, and Demas send greetings. 15 Give my greetings to the brothers at Laodicea, and to Nympha and the church in her*

> house. **16** *After this letter has been read to you, see that it is also read in the church of the Laodiceans and that you in turn read the letter from Laodicea.* **17** *Tell Archippus: "See to it that you complete the work you have received in the Lord."* **18** *I, Paul, write this greeting in my own hand. Remember my chains. Grace be with you. (Colossians 4:2-18)*

This chapter is filled with as many takeaway applications as there are names of people and requests and commands specific to them. Each of these takeaways serves as a stimulus, or reminder, or rebuke or further lesson within our personal training as disciples of Jesus Christ. I will highlight all of them. After giving the Colossians some counsel for living within relationships at home and at work at the end of Chapter 3 and the first verse of chapter four, Paul talks to the Colossians about prayer, 4:2-4.

Persevere In Prayer And Pray For Effective Gospel Proclamation.

In a December 4, 2006 online Q&A session offered by the UK's The Independent, atheist Richard Dawkins was asked the following question: "If you died and arrived at the gates of heaven, what would you say to God to justify your lifelong atheism?" His response was, "I'd quote Bertrand Russell: 'Not enough evidence, God! Not enough evidence!'"

Lack of evidence is insufficient reason for leaping to atheism. The reasonable conclusion might be agnosticism but not an emphatic 'there is no god' position. People who espouse atheism find difficulty in wrapping their minds around the idea of a preexistent God, who has been living as it were, before there was a universe in which the atheists' planet earth revolved around a sun. Atheists discard the thesis that out of a vacuum, God spoke forth the generation of light and star-studded galaxies, and oceans, and land and vegetation, and living creatures on land and in the water and the sky. Atheists certainly do not believe that God climaxed his creation with the formation of a creature with personhood and soul and with capacity to intelligently interact with God. Atheists refuse to believe that this relationship with God was interrupted by human sin that infected the nature of the entire human race.

It is an enormous step of faith for a human to move from non-belief to belief because it requires intellectual acknowledgment that God who is infinite but invisible can be known. The Bible informs us that God remained invisible for countless generations yet allowed some humans to know him when he took the initiative to communicate with those specific people. Those disclosures provided glimpses of who God is and what are his expectations of the human creatures who inhabit earth. As vague as their concept may have been, people began to believe in God. When Jesus was born on earth, God made himself visible in an exceptional manner. God became flesh and lived here among our kind. Paul told the Colossians in chapter one, verse 15 that Jesus is the image of the invisible God and that he created all things and everything was created through him and for him. Jesus became incarnate God in order to fulfill a redemptive purpose of reconciling his spoiled creation to himself and his redemptive action required his blood on a cross. Each person who takes this giant step of faith, establishes a relationship with the true God, and is instantly impressed with the enormity of the privilege of communicating with God? Commonplace, unremarkable humans such as each we are, can speak to God, knowing that we are permitted to regard him as 'Father,' and to assume that he is intimately near. Jesus encouraged his followers to employ this privilege of communicating with God, his Father in heaven. The supremely powerful God, who created this universe that we are only capable of exploring superficially, permits you and me to talk with him. The Bible teaches that prayer is foundational to our lives as Christians.

Although Christians in Colossae had learned to pray, if they experienced what many of us have sometimes exhibited, they also neglected prayer or displaced prayer for other more entertaining activities, like googling, facebooking and emailing. So Paul spurs them on with an apropos Greek word, "proskartereo," which means, "continue" but in the sense of "be earnest towards prayer, or persevere at praying, be constantly diligent about praying." Prayer truly is a discipline requiring us to be earnest enough to schedule it into our calendars and to keep to the schedule.

> *2 Devote yourselves to prayer, being watchful and thankful. 3 And pray for us, too, that God may open a door for our message, so that we may proclaim the mystery of Christ, for which I am in chains. 4 Pray that I may proclaim it clearly, as I should. (Colossians 4:2-4)*

Being watchful or alert while praying implies that prayer is not a monologue. God may communicate with us during prayer. We must be expectant and waiting to hear from God. We may hear from God by way of a thought, a quiet Holy Spirit impression, or a verse that we read. Paul reminds us of the thanksgiving component to prayer which effectively prevents us from allowing our prayer lives from becoming a litany of 'poor me' complaints. I picked up somewhere, the 'sandwich' model for prayer, in which we only express our hurts and needs between thanksgiving, so it's one slice of thanksgiving, then the expression of concerns and requests and then another slice of thanksgiving.

Paul asks the believers to "pray for us", by which I assume he meant others beside himself, perhaps referring to everyone whom he names in vss 7,8, and 9; Tychicus, Onesimus, Aristarchus, Justus (Jesus), Epaphras, Luke and Demas. These people were members of his support team who encouraged him and looked after some of his personal needs.

Their own faithful witness was a testimony to Christ. He asks for prayer that a door will open and he is not speaking about the prison door but rather a door of opportunity for preaching the gospel. Whereas I have called his message the 'gospel,' Paul called it 'the mystery of Christ', and for good reason. The citizens of Colossae were influenced by proponents of so-called mystery religions that boasted spiritual secrets. Paul capitalized upon this, saying that the mystery of God has been revealed in Jesus Christ. Jesus is the mystery of God. Intellectuals, cynics, scoffers took exception to him, yet here he was asking Colossians to ask God to give him further opportunities to speak about the revealed mystery regardless of any consequences. Paul wanted to be able speak for God plainly and convincingly even from where he was in prison. For decades in North America we thought that or acted as though evangelism was done within the walls of the church building. I have seen a shift in our understanding. Evangelism is effected everywhere that believers use opportunities to speak good news all week long. The first takeaway is, persevere in prayer and pray for effective gospel proclamation.

Be Opportunistically Ready To Share Your Faith

4 Pray that I may proclaim it clearly, as I should. 5 Be wise in the way you act toward outsiders; make the most of every opportunity. 6 Let your conversation be always full of grace, seasoned with salt, so that you may know how to answer everyone. (Colossians 4;5,6)

When Paul speaks to Christians about "outsiders" he is referring to unbelievers. Rather than avoiding outsiders, Paul encourages prudent conduct when Christians interact with unbelievers. Christians should regard such interface as opportunity that they do their utmost not to squander. Since Paul's comment serves as another takeaway for us, we must use the time judiciously, making the best use of that time that you have to convey the good news. When conversation occurs, it should be notably gracious and seasoned with salt. People who see Jesus mirrored in you make inquiries. Grabbing people by the collar and demanding that they listen to you is unnecessary. They do have interest. They are fascinated curious about your certainty. The appetite for truth is bumped up by your skillful and tasteful references to the love of Jesus. Ask God to help us to recognize open doors, to follow-up on timid inquiries and to bring those who are attracted to Jesus into a life of faith.

I initially objected to the lyrics contained in a Christian song. "Jesus is the only way, but there's more than one way to Jesus." It sounded blasphemous but then I realized it is true. Not all religions make valid statements about god religions. There are not many ways to God. There is one way to the Father. *"There is no other name under heaven that has been given among men, by which we must be saved"* (Acts 4:12). However, there is more than one way to Jesus. Some people come to faith as children, some by reading, by logic, by debate, through fear, and through desperation. Christians are called to enter the world of outsiders, prepared, knowing what to say and how to say it; what not to say; how to listen; and how to be gracious, wise, clear, and courageous as we share the words of eternal life, the "mystery of Christ."

That's an apt portrayal of lifestyle evangelism, which is not new but was promoted as early as the first century. Paul says to Colossians and to us, that we cannot wait for special meetings with advertised times. Here is evangelism in the course of daily activities. Even in prison Paul will live out the gospel. Jesus himself was an opportunist, meeting Bartimaeus, a blind man beside the road, and a demonic man from Gadara whom he met on a seashore, and Zaccheus, a squirt of a man with whom he spent a lunchtime and Matthew's friends with whom he enjoyed a supper meal.

God in the Open

Jesus knew how to speak to and to answer every person with whom he had a conversation. This is the lesson, that we should know how to answer each person and that we should be opportunistically ready to share our faith.

Paul begins a citation of people whom he regards highly and commends to the Colossians. The reasons for his esteem provide us with other takeaways. The churches knew whom he was talking about but we know almost nothing about most of the people whose names Paul drops in these next 17 verses. The first person mentioned is a man named Tychicus, whom together with Onesimus Paul introduces as those who will bring this letter to them and inform them about Paul's welfare. Paul considers Tychicus to be central to the Colossians' spiritual welfare.

Establish A Track Reputation for Being Spiritual And Reliable.

7 Tychicus will tell you all the news about me. He is a dear brother, a faithful minister and fellow servant in the Lord. 8 I am sending him to you for the express purpose that you may know about our circumstances and that he may encourage your hearts. 9 He is coming with Onesimus, our faithful and dear brother, who is one of you. They will tell you everything that is happening here. (Colossians 4:7-9)

A concise narration about Tychicus develops from references about him in Acts, Ephesians, 2 Timothy and Titus. Tychicus came from the Roman province known as Asia Minor, where, in the city of Corinth, he joined Paul during Paul's last missionary journey. Tychicus became a Christian and remained with Paul for many years. Tychicus may have been a resident of Corinth although some tradition suggests he was from Ephesus. Together with Trophimus, Tychicus accompanied the Apostle Paul on his journey from Macedonia to Jerusalem. He was also with Paul in Rome during Paul's incarceration, which had two stages, one was house arrest and the other was actual imprisonment. In between those sentences, Paul had personal freedom and of course he continued his gospel preaching. Tychicus was a continuous help and cheerleader to Paul in Rome. Like any true mentor, Paul recognized giftedness in Tychicus and at one point sent him to Ephesus to relieve Timothy. This permitted Timothy, who was a fulltime worker in Ephesus, to visit Paul in Rome. Tychicus went on to serve as a teacher, pastor and a mentor. He was deemed trustworthy enough to be a transitional pastor. Paul wrote to Titus intimating that he may send Tychicus to Crete where Titus was in charge of several churches. This allowed Titus to join Paul for a while. In this letter to Colossian we are told that Paul sent Tychicus to Colossae probably carrying this letter. Paul regards him as far more than a courier, but as someone who can also answer all their questions about Paul's imprisonment so that they can pray more effectively for him as he has asked them to do. Beyond this I believe that Paul wanted Tychicus to be his designate to continue the pastoral/teaching ministry at least in Colossae during Paul's imprisonment. It might have seemed that Epaphras who was mentioned earlier in the letter, would have been the natural person for that ministry since he first brought the gospel to Colossae and was himself a Colossian citizen but there is a suggestion that Epaphras' relationship with the Colossians was troubled and required some intervention. In 4:12-13 Paul appears to be reassuring the Church about Epaphras, reminding them about his sincerity and faithfulness and hard work on their behalf. So with his plans for Tychicus in mind, Paul writes this rousing endorsement that Tychicus is a beloved brother and a faithful minister and a fellow servant of the Lord. They are all titles that mean he is a valued colleague and made of the right stuff to give oversight to work in Colossae.

Verse 9 mentions Onesimus who accompanied Tychicus on this occasion of delivering the letter, and the Church is reminded that he is

God in the Open

actually one of them, a Colossian, and someone worth knowing well and listening to because he too is assessed by Paul as a faithful and beloved brother. A further and fuller treatment of Onesimus comes in the next chapter when we examine the short letter from Paul to Philemon. His is an awesome story.

Imagine what it was like when the Christian faith was new, and the movement so fledgling and exciting, and the primary names that are mentioned here were all people who knew one another and sometimes travelled together with Paul. Many churches in various regions knew them, whereas we read about them as single names detached from any connected story. We can hear the collegiality and solidarity in Acts 20:1-6.

> *1 When the uproar had ended, Paul sent for the disciples and, after encouraging them, said good-by and set out for Macedonia. 2 He traveled through that area, speaking many words of encouragement to the people, and finally arrived in Greece, 3 where he stayed three months. Because the Jews made a plot against him just as he was about to sail for Syria, he decided to go back through Macedonia. 4 He was accompanied by Sopater son of Pyrrhus from Berea, Aristarchus and Secundus from Thessalonica, Gaius from Derbe, Timothy also, and Tychicus and Trophimus from the province of Asia. 5 These men went on ahead and waited for us at Troas. 6 But we sailed from Philippi after the Feast of Unleavened Bread, and five days later joined the others at Troas, where we stayed seven days. (Acts 20:1-6)*

Resolve To Be Faithful So Your Life Is An Inspiration To Others.

> *10 My fellow prisoner Aristarchus sends you his greetings, as does Mark, the cousin of Barnabas. (Colossians 4:10)*

We know little about Aristarchus in Colossians but the book of Acts tells us a great deal about Aristarchus. It seems Paul is assuming the Colossians already know about him. This was a wonderful man, with unrivalled dedication to the LORD.

Aristarchus was a Greek Macedonian from the City of Thessalonica and he was one of the early Christian converts during Paul's trip to Thessalonica (Acts 17). He was trustworthy as is attested by the responsibility Paul gave him when sending him from Thessalonica with money intended for the care of the poor in Jerusalem. He was also physically strong and could travel. He accompanied Paul across the Roman Empire. Together with Gaius, another Macedonian convert, he went with Paul on his third missionary journey, most likely travelling to Athens and Corinth before heading to Ephesus where because Paul taught that idols were worthless, he infuriated the idol manufacturers and merchants who started a riot. People stormed the streets, screamed death threats and attempted to kill the Christians. Acts 19:24-31. They were mobbed and seized and taken into custody into the great Theatre there. My wife Christine and I, like many tourists, have stood in the remains of that theatre without walls. Aristarchus was one of those who stood by Paul in the thick of it. He was the kind of person you want to have with you when you have trouble. Their lives were spared.

Despite what happened in Ephesus, Aristarchus continued with Paul through Macedonia and Achaia, experiencing severe opposition, attempts by Jews to stop his mission, Acts 20:3,7). Later he accompanied Paul on the prison ship from Caesarea to Rome, where Paul was imprisoned at the time of this writing. In verse 10 Paul calls him "my fellow prisoner, so he certainly needs the Colossians to pray for him, so that he too will be able to make the mystery of Christ clear and to use every opportunity even though he is in prison with Paul." He shared Paul's two-year imprisonment with him. "*When two years had passed, Felix was succeeded by Porcius Festus, but because Felix wanted to grant a favor to the Jews, he left Paul in prison"* (Acts 24:27). He was a brother you could count on; he hung with the apostle, lived under the same circumstances, and served his good friend because he cared about him.

Aristarchus' courage was nothing short of Paul's. Few of us are cut out to be Paul. While being a Paul is a great thing, let us be content with being an Aristarchus, a Christian who didn't let trials and tribulations discourage him, but pressed toward the goal. We have caught a brief glimpse of a faithful Christian, whose conduct can be an inspiration for us. A faithful Christian is not necessarily one who is remembered or recognized by most men for their conduct and good works, but by God. The man stayed the course regardless of the opposition. He accompanied Paul back to Jerusalem. Resolve to be faithful no matter what, so your daily life is an inspiration to others.

Mark and Jesus Justus are mentioned together as being fellow workers with Paul for the Kingdom of God. Yet the surprising comment is that they are Jews, which is the reference to the circumcision, yet they are the only Jews in the city of Rome, who have remained supportive of Paul and willing to identify publicly with Kingdom work.

> ***10*** *My fellow prisoner Aristarchus sends you his greetings, as does Mark, the cousin of Barnabas. (You have received instructions about him; if he comes to you, welcome him.)* ***11*** *Jesus, who is called Justus, also sends greetings. These are the only Jews among my fellow workers for the kingdom of God, and they have proved a comfort to me. (Colossians 4:10-11)*

Mark was the cousin of Barnabas. Colossians have been asked to welcome warmly Mark warmly if he comes their way. In order to appreciate Mark, let us compare and contrast him with Demas who is mentioned in verse 14. "*Our dear friend Luke, the doctor, and Demas send greetings.*" Have you ever heard of Demas? Demas appears here to be in

Paul's good books. That changes. There are other informative references to Demas.

Prioritize Unconditional Service To Christ Rather Than To The World.

A native of Thessalonica, Demas had probably never heard about Jesus until the apostle Paul, then in his fifties, arrived in Demas' home city, talking about some crazy events that recently took place in Judea. Furnished with a touch of imagination, I picture Demas as an agreeable, pleasant young man, a non-believer, who was drawn to Paul and his compelling stories about a new way of life and Jesus, the Son of God. Daily, he sat listening to Paul's exceptional teaching. Demas professed to believe in Jesus Christ. He became affected with the enthusiasm of new faith and the exhilaration of a cause for which he was willing to risk himself just as his new mentor was doing. He wanted to live and die with Paul. Demas began well. We can read Demas' name among Paul's early companions. *"Epaphras, my fellow prisoner in Christ Jesus, sends you his greetings. So do Mark, Aristarchus, Demas, and Luke, my co-workers"* (Philemon 1:23-24). Demas was there with Paul at the beginning when Christianity began to take hold at the far reaches of the Roman empire. Demas was given a greater opportunity to impact the world for Jesus than most people in history. Even here in Colossians, after Paul praised Mark, Epaphras, and Aristarchus, he mentioned Demas and it appears that all is still well. *"Luke, the beloved doctor, sends his greetings, and so does Demas"* (Colossians 4:14).

However, Demas' character and loyalty became suspect at one stage in his life. The suspicion became a crippling handicap. Demas came with Paul to the great city of Rome, the capital of the world. Paul's

God in the Open

preaching stirred controversy and Demas was with Paul in Rome during Paul's first imprisonment. Four or five years later, he was with Paul and Epaphras who were again prisoners but he himself was not a prisoner. There in the renowned city surrounded by opulence, the magnificent architecture, the decorated halls of the Caesars, the elegant residences, the aromas of culinary and vineyard delights, the new world of music and comedy and decadent loves, he became entranced and he acceded to its attraction. While his friends languished in prison, he ignored them and the gospel for the ecstasy of the great city and all that it offered. Evidenced in Paul's second letter to Timothy, Paul knows that he is running out of earthly time so he exhorts Timothy to take up the mantle of preaching and to fulfill all that God has called him to be and to do. Paul feels as though his own life is being poured out like a liquid offering. With an anguished kind of plea Paul says, *"do your best to come to me soon. For Demas, in love with this present world, has deserted me and gone to Thessalonica"*, (2 Tim 4:9,10). That must have been one of Paul's most heartbreaking lines. There is no record of Demas having been restored.

Forgive Someone Who Has Recovered From A Fault And Forget It.

Mark, on the other hand, gives us hope. He had a weak start and Mark didn't appear to have the right stuff. He disappointed his leaders and his friends but Mark finished well. During the early days of his discipleship and gospel work, during the first missionary trip with Paul and Barnabas, Mark took off from Pamphylia and returned to his home in Jerusalem (Acts 13:13). That was unfortunate and troubling because he left his comrades to bear the heat of the spiritual battle without him. We don't know why, but Paul did not approve. In fact, when Barnabas wanted to bring Mark back on the team after the Jerusalem Council, Paul refused to consider it.

129

> *37 Barnabas wanted to take John, also called Mark, with them, 38 but Paul did not think it wise to take him, because he had deserted them in Pamphylia and had not continued with them in the work. 39 They had such a sharp disagreement that they parted company. Barnabas took Mark and sailed for Cyprus, 40 but Paul chose Silas and left, commended by the brothers to the grace of the Lord. (Acts 15:37-40)*

Later, Mark rejoined the battle and proved to be a faithful, trusted, useful warrior and companion. What is truly stunning is the change of mind that Paul had about Mark because in that same 2 Timothy 4 passage in which Paul revealed that Demas had deserted Paul and maybe even the gospel, he told Timothy in verse 11, *"Get Mark and bring him with you for he is very useful to me for ministry."* Even after Paul was gone, the Lord used Mark to contribute a gospel to the New Testament canon. He traveled all over Italy preaching the good news before he sailed for Egypt where he died or was martyred.

Comfort Your Friends with Whom You Share Jesus' Name.

> *11 Jesus, who is called Justus, also sends greetings. These are the only Jews among my fellow workers for the kingdom of God, and they have proved a comfort to me.* (Colossians 4:11)

Here was a man called Justus, sometimes known as Jesus. Jesus Justus is not mentioned elsewhere in the New Testament, and nothing more is known about him than what is given in this verse in Colossians, namely, that he was by birth a Jew, "of the circumcision." He converted to faith in Christ and he was one of the inner circle of intimate friends and associates of the apostle Paul during his first Roman captivity. Aristarchus, Mark and Justus were the only Jewish men in his company of kingdom workers, and Paul has received much comfort from them. Jesus Justus was one of this small minority who, when the going became tough for Paul, these had remained loyal and available to Paul. Likely this praise comes at the time that Paul found that not only did the Roman populace and military harass him, but also the Christians there had themselves grown weary of him or seen him as a risk. They feared persecution and his preaching fomented animosity, so they withdrew from him. This defection did not come from the Gentile believers at Rome but from the Jewish segment and that is why Paul's comment is striking, Justus however did not cast him off. *"These are the only Jews among my fellow workers for the kingdom of God, and they have proved a comfort to me."*

Intercede For Those Whom You Lead, So They Will Become Spiritually Mature.

> *12 Epaphras, who is one of you and a servant of Christ Jesus, sends greetings. He is always wrestling in prayer for you, that you may stand firm in all the will of God, mature and fully assured. 13 I vouch for him that he is working hard for you and for those at Laodicea and Hierapolis. (Colossians 4:12-13)*

Epaphras is mentioned as a fellow Colossian, a native of Colossae, "one of your number," who is presently with Paul in Rome. From Rome, he also sends his greetings by Paul's letter. Epaphras was the one who founded the church in Colossae after he went to Ephesus, heard the gospel, and met Christ. Epaphras is considered a servant of Christ Jesus, and is always struggling on behalf of the Colossians through his prayers. Epaphras was someone who spent hours bringing heaven and earth together in his prayers. Epaphras prays that the believers will stand fully mature and completely confident in the will of God. Paul commends Epaphras for his hard work on behalf of Colossians as well as their sister cities of the Tri-City area, Laodicea and Hierapolis.

Record What God Is Doing So You Can Tell Others How Good And Personal God Is.

> **14** *Our dear friend Luke, the doctor, and Demas send greetings. (Colossians 4:14)*

Luke was not Jewish but since his conversion he remained with Paul through some of the most awesome moments of church history as well as some of the most frightening. Luke is mentioned as the much-loved physician who because he is with Paul, also greets the Colossians from Rome. Luke was the team physician. It was a significant benefit to Paul and the others and it must have been reassuring to have the company of someone who knew what to do with a broken bone, or to reduce a fever, or to treat torn skin tissue. Paul rejoiced to have somebody with him who could care for people's physical needs. All the time that Luke was performing those duties he was watching and listening to everyone, putting himself in the background but taking notes. He ended up giving us perhaps the greatest history ever penned by anyone, the two-volume set of the gospel of Luke and the book of Acts.

Whatever You Have, Make It Available For God To Use.

Paul mentions Nympha and a letter exchange.

> **15** *Give my greetings to the brothers at Laodicea, and to Nympha and the church in her house.* **16** *After this letter has been read to you, see that it is also read in the church of the Laodiceans and that you in turn read the letter from Laodicea. (Colossians 4:15,16)*

Most scholars agree that the original document said Nympha was a woman who owned a home and was giving leadership and hospitality to this church. But scribes transcribing the Bible changed it from a feminine name to a masculine name, because of their discomfort with women in prominent positions in the church. The King James version (KJV) of the Bible states the verse as follows: *"Salute the brethren which are in*

Laodicea, and Nymphas, and the church which is in his house." However, more recent translations refer to Nympha (no final "s"), and thus, a female appellation. Paul wants a greeting to be passed to the Laodiceans and to Nympha and all who comprise the church that meets in her house (Colossians 4:15). She had a home and it was open and available to the LORD for his purposes. Tell God you are available for whatever, wherever and whenever.

Paul requested that the Laodiceans, perhaps meeting in the house church of Nympha (there is no mention of a husband, father, or brother), read the letter openly in church. He also advised the Colossian Christians to read the letter from Laodicea. That letter may have been written by Paul, but is now lost. There is no Greek text for a Laodicean letter, and that was a decisive reason for rejecting the authenticity of several ancient texts that were purported to be the missing "Epistle to the Laodiceans." The other New Testament books and letters all have ancient Greek manuscripts. There is however one ancient Latin manuscript entitled "Epistle to the Laodiceans", which turns out to be in actuality a brief compilation of verses from other Pauline epistles, principally Philippians. Scholarly opinion is divided as to whether it is a forgery or an orthodox copy of something earlier. It is generally considered a "clumsy forgery" and an attempt to seek to answer the "riddle" created by the reference in Colossians 4:16.

Even If No One Knows Your Name, Soldier On To Complete Your Work For Christ.

Archippus is one of the many little known Christians who served Christ and whom Paul greeted in two passages of scripture, Colossians 4:17 and Philemon 1:2.

> *17 Tell Archippus: "See to it that you complete the work you have received in the Lord." (Colossians 4:17)*

In Colossians Paul exhorted Archippus to fulfill the ministry that God had given him. It can be surmised that he preached in the church at Colossae. We cannot come to a firm conclusion about what ministry that was, but we do know that he was to give all diligence to follow it out fully. In Philemon 1:2 Paul writes, "*Paul, a prisoner for Christ Jesus and Timothy our brother, to Philemon our beloved fellow worker and Apphia our sister and Archippus our fellow soldier and the church in your house.*" Paul called him a "*fellow worker*" and a "*fellow soldier*" and that indicates a strong participation in gospel and church leadership.

> *18 I, Paul, write this greeting in my own hand. Remember my chains. Grace be with you. (Colossians 4:18)*

With the words, "Grace be with you," Colossians closes as it began, in celebration of God's grace. "*To the holy and faithful brothers in Christ at Colossae: Grace and peace to you from God our Father* (Colossians 1:2). Paul's crowning words for his church of any district and any age assert that God's empowering grace is with the church, in the certain confidence that those who have participated in God's salvation with Christ will be sustained to the end (Rom. 8:28-39).

> *28 And we know that in all things God works for the good of those who love him, who have been called according to his purpose. 29 For those God foreknew he also predestined to be conformed to the likeness of his Son, that he might be the firstborn among many brothers. 30 And those he predestined, he also called; those he called, he also justified; those he justified, he also glorified. 31 What, then, shall we say in response to this? If God is for us, who can be against us? 32 He who did not spare his own Son, but gave him up for us all--how will he not also, along with him, graciously give us all things? 33 Who will bring any charge against those whom God has chosen? It is God who justifies. 34 Who is he that*

*condemns? Christ Jesus, who died--more than that, who was raised to life--is at the right hand of God and is also interceding for us. **35** Who shall separate us from the love of Christ? Shall trouble or hardship or persecution or famine or nakedness or danger or sword? **36** As it is written: "For your sake we face death all day long; we are considered as sheep to be slaughtered." **37** No, in all these things we are more than conquerors through him who loved us. **38** For I am convinced that neither death nor life, neither angels nor demons, neither the present nor the future, nor any powers, **39** neither height nor depth, nor anything else in all creation, will be able to separate us from the love of God that is in Christ Jesus our Lord. (Romans 8:28-39)*

Chapter Eight

ONESIMUS

Paul's letter to Philemon is an intersection of several life stories. The principal figures of their shared narrative are Paul, Philemon and Onesimus. Secondary characters are Apphia and Archippus, and incidental players are Timothy, Epaphras, Mark, Aristarchus, Demas and Luke. All of these are referenced in this short New Testament letter consisting of twenty-five verses.

An examination of Philemon is a natural postscript to a study of Colossians because both Philemon and Onesimus lived in Colossae. Paul's letters to Colossians and to Philemon were penned at the same time. Philemon was a citizen of Colossae, a wealthy, noble and charitable man who possessed slaves. His house was the Downton Abbey of Colossae and he extended hospitality to many people. By the grace of God Philemon was converted most probably through his acquaintance with Paul during the years that Paul was in residence in Ephesus, since Paul never visited Colossae. Philemon became a valued personal friend of Paul. Philemon's home became a place of meeting and worship for Christians and he himself became active in Gospel proclamation. *"Paul, a prisoner of Christ Jesus, and Timothy our brother, To Philemon our dear friend and fellow worker."* (Philemon 1)

The first mention of Onesimus in this letter is in verse 10 in which Paul begins his appeal on this man's behalf. *"I appeal to you for my son Onesimus, who became my son while I was in chains."* For reasons unknown, Onesimus became a slave to Philemon of Colossae. Perhaps Onesimus was born into slavery. Perhaps he was a prisoner of war. Perhaps

God in the Open

he had become so deeply in debt that he had no option but to sell himself into slavery. Roman law and culture supported the practice of slavery. I will not examine or debate the ethics and morality of slavery here, because Paul, the author of the letter doesn't do that.

My purpose is to creatively retell one slave's story while reviewing Paul's letter to the slave owner. We will learn to what extent God's transformation of two people's personal lives can redeem their relationship with one another after it was ruptured and ill will and bad feelings were generated. This should teach us how God's grace can be expected to alter our attitudes towards people whom we have wronged, or people who have wronged us.

This is a powerful, dramatic plot line that I do not want you to miss, so to begin, I will employ a liberal amount of pleasurable imagination while using the available information and the historical context to tell my version of this plausible scenario, this great story. Then I will spend some time examining the text of the letter.

First, The Narrative - Le Miserable No Longer

For some time now, Onesimus had been considering taking off. It would be easy. He was not in chains and there were no high fences around the estate. The risks however were high. If he left his master, he would be a fugitive on the run. If he were found, Roman law allowed his master to have him flogged, even put to death. Philemon had many slaves but Onesimus did not discuss his thoughts and plans with any of them. All the others seemed resigned to their conditions. Onesimus had served Philemon as his slave for several years already. Philemon was not a despotic master. In fact, Philemon was a Christian now and that had brought a change. Onesimus remembered accompanying Philemon on a business trip to Ephesus where his master met the religious man named Paul who was living in Ephesus. The entire Lycus Valley was talking about Paul, even Onesimus' fellow slaves knew about him and wanted to see him.

Paul preached about Jesus from Nazareth, the prophet who had been crucified. Many people believed that Jesus was the Son of God. Onesimus witnessed that Philemon had some kind of religious experience in Ephesus and Philemon and Paul had become friends. From then on, even Onesimus observed that his master was more considerate of his slaves than other masters were, but slavery is slavery. Onesimus was a young man and he could not imagine spending more of his life like this. He would not let that happen to himself. One aspect of his duties gave him access to some of his master's funds. He had skimmed a bit of that for many weeks and secreted it away for himself. Now on the eve of his intended flight from Colossae he took a substantial amount of money. He slept lightly and at three o'clock in the morning, long before the roosters or the sun were up, he took his bag with his paltry belongings and left.

He wasn't sure where he was heading. Freedom was good enough. He was a free man, able to choose what he would do, where he would go and he had some cash to make the trip manageable. As dangerous as night travel was along the roads, he did most of his early travel from Colossae to Ephesus at night to avoid bounty hunters whom Philemon may have set on his trail. He should be able to get lost among 300,000 people yet he felt it was unsafe to stay in Ephesus very long so after two nights, he booked passage on a boat that made numerous port stops but seven weeks later he arrived at the western shore of the Italian boot, four days walk from Rome. The passage had cost more money than he wanted to spend but he wanted to get as far away from his past as he could. He had succeeded in doing that.

So here he was in the empire's greatest city with so much to see, but the city intimidated him. The Roman military presence was everywhere. The artistry and ostentatious architecture were treats to his eyes, yet made him so nervous he longed for the country. Whatever he thought he might experience upon his arrival in Rome, reality was much different. Almost penniless, wearing the brand of a slave, still feeling the need to hide, feeling lost and afraid, and knowing that having stolen that money, a death sentence was a possibility, he became a street person. He spent many days and nights like this. Then in stilted conversation with other beggars, he heard that Paul, the travelling spiritual man with whom his master Philemon had established a friendship, was there in Rome. However, Paul was a prisoner, placed under house arrest. Having nowhere to go and no one that he could trust, Onesimus began asking about and looking for Paul. He found the rental home where Paul was staying and fortunately Paul was inclined to receive anyone who came to him. Inside the house were others, helpers who seemed to attend to Paul's needs and his guests' needs, preparing meals, reading to him, some times writing down what he told them, other times sitting and listening to him teach.

They whispered to Paul about the presence of this new guest. Paul looked over at Onesimus but didn't recognize him. He gave instructions to the others concerning him. They fed Onesimus and let him rest there in a corner, but soon, in front of the other occupants, Paul asked Onesimus to come to sit beside him and to tell about himself, who he was, why he was in Rome and why he had come to this house. Onesimus was apprehensive. He didn't know whom he could trust. He didn't know whether someone there might report him. Sensing this unease, Paul told his own story. The others in the house had heard Paul's story many times before but it was always stirring and Paul never embellished it but spoke it humbly and gratefully.

He told how he was a well-educated Jew who became infuriated by Christianity. Even after Jesus had been put to death, his disciples were claiming that Jesus was the Son of God and that he had come back to life and then had been taken up into heaven and that he was going to return. They were preaching that all who put their trust in Jesus as Son of God and believed that when Jesus died, he had made atonement for human sin, would be completely forgiven of sin and become new persons. Paul emphatically expressed how unsound and stupid he had believed those ideas to be. Furthermore, he formerly believed that the teaching posed a threat to the Jewish community because so many people believed that Jesus really was the promised Messiah of God. Taking the initiative, Paul had received authorization from the Synagogue to arrest Christians and slap them into jail. Some were even put to death. On the day that he was walking to Damascus to clean out Christians there, he had been temporarily blinded, rendered sightless by an intense light overhead, and the voice of Jesus spoke with him, telling him that all these actions against Christians was actually persecuting him, Jesus. There in that temporary house prison, Paul told Onesimus how in the days that followed, Jesus gave Paul a new assignment, to preach for him to the Gentile world and that he had been doing this ever since.

Onesimus asked Paul all the questions that any of us might ask about faith and he heard the answers that told him what he could expect. Paul said that the experience is like being blind and suddenly being able to see, like being lost and suddenly being found. Paul said he had been a free man, but he was now content to spend the rest of his life as a slave, a servant of Jesus Christ. When Paul mentioned the word "slave,' Onesimus stammered and said, "Alright, I'll tell you about myself," and he explained to the household who he was and what he had done. When Onesimus mentioned Philemon's name, Paul's eyebrows lifted in recognition of his friend in Colossae and Paul listened fervently to the story.

When Onesimus had completed his tale, Paul said to him. *"I want to tell you some things that Jesus said when he was here on earth. Jewish scribes and Pharisees were cynics just as I was, and were always trying to accuse him. He told them, 'I am going away and you will look for me and you will not find me and you will die in your sin because where I am going you cannot come.' They wondered if he was going to commit suicide right there but then he said. 'You are from below. I am from above. You are from this world. I am not of this world. I told you that you would die in your sins, for unless you believe that I am he, you will die in your sins.'"* (John 8: 21-23)

Paul put this to Onesimus, "You don't want to die in your sin, do you?"

Onesimus offered, "No."

Paul said, "Jesus told everyone that unless you believe in him you will die in your sin."

Onesimus, noticeably emotional, shaking, anxious about these fanatics and yet curiously drawn by their undeniable confidence, was hesitating. Then Paul said, "Jesus also said on that occasion, 'If you abide in my word, you are truly my disciples, and you will know the truth and the truth will set you free. Truly, truly, I say to you, everyone who commits sin is a slave to sin. The slave does not remain in the house forever; the son remains forever. So if the Son sets you free, you will be free indeed.'"

Onesimus exclaimed, "I want that! I want the Son to set me free, to be really free, completely free, definitely free."

Paul said to him, "Then believe on the Lord Jesus Christ, and you will be saved."

That was the day that Onesimus became a Christian. He was given permission to stay in this safe house because Paul wanted him to learn as much as possible about the mystery of God which is Jesus Christ, the image of the invisible God, the one who is creator of all things and who sustains all things and who is absolutely supreme, and who is seated right now at the right hand of the Father above. Paul wanted Onesimus to understand how when faith is placed in Jesus, there is an immediate investment of that person's identity in the death of Christ and the resurrection of Christ and life is so integrally tied to Jesus that a person is able to look at life through Jesus' eyes and to respond to life's challenges and opportunities and relationships as Jesus would.

Onesimus could not remember any time in his life that he had felt any better than he did in the days that followed. He truly felt like a new man. He learned to talk with God. He believed his life had purpose. All these strangers had become family to him in such short time. After about 30 days of such teaching, Paul had a private conversation with Onesimus, and told him that he believed that it would be prudent and proper for Onesimus to return to his former master and to confess his theft and to make things right regardless of the feared consequences. In order to mitigate this worrisome step, Paul would write a personal letter to Philemon and he would send Onesimus to deliver the letter in person. "Are you up to this Onesimus?" Paul asked. The answer was affirmative and Paul acknowledged this with a grand smile and said, "Stay for a while longer and work with me,' and for a couple of months Onesimus provided useful service to Paul just as the other houseguests did. Paul genuinely liked the young man, valued him but now it was time to release him to their agreed upon plan.

Onesimus' Journey Of Reconciliation

The return itself was difficult, travelling 1481 miles by foot, boat and pack horse with the full understanding that the man to whom he was returning had legal authority to kill him on the spot or to maim him, or to brand him on the forehead. What could Paul possibly say in a letter that would effectively heal the breach between Philemon and Onesimus? What could Paul write that would dissuade Philemon from exercising his lawful prerogative of demanding justice? What reasons could he present to persuade Philemon to accept Onesimus? Philemon stood unsmiling, holding the letter that had been handed to him, facing Onesimus, who knelt before him with head bowed. Philemon unwound the letter and scrolled it open and then he read.

> *1 Paul, a prisoner of Christ Jesus, and Timothy our brother, To Philemon our dear friend and fellow worker, 2 to Apphia our sister, to Archippus our fellow soldier and to the church that meets in your home: 3 Grace to you and peace from God our Father and the Lord Jesus Christ.*
> *Thanksgiving and Prayer*
> *4 I always thank my God as I remember you in my prayers, 5 because I hear about your faith in the Lord Jesus and your love for all the saints. 6 I pray that you may be active in sharing your faith, so that you will have a full understanding of every good thing we have in Christ. 7 Your love has given me great joy and encouragement, because you, brother, have refreshed the hearts of the saints.*
> *Paul's Plea for Onesimus*
> *8 Therefore, although in Christ I could be bold and order you to do what you ought to do, 9 yet I appeal to you on the basis of love. I then, as Paul--an old man and now also a prisoner of Christ Jesus-- 10 I appeal to you for my son Onesimus, who became my*

> son while I was in chains. 11 Formerly he was useless to you, but now he has become useful both to you and to me. 12 I am sending him--who is my very heart--back to you. 13 I would have liked to keep him with me so that he could take your place in helping me while I am in chains for the gospel. 14 But I did not want to do anything without your consent, so that any favor you do will be spontaneous and not forced. 15 Perhaps the reason he was separated from you for a little while was that you might have him back for good-- 16 no longer as a slave, but better than a slave, as a dear brother. He is very dear to me but even dearer to you, both as a man and as a brother in the Lord. 17 So if you consider me a partner, welcome him as you would welcome me. 18 If he has done you any wrong or owes you anything, charge it to me. 19 I, Paul, am writing this with my own hand. I will pay it back--not to mention that you owe me your very self. 20 I do wish, brother, that I may have some benefit from you in the Lord; refresh my heart in Christ. 21 Confident of your obedience, I write to you, knowing that you will do even more than I ask. 22 And one thing more: Prepare a guest room for me, because I hope to be restored to you in answer to your prayers. 23 Epaphras, my fellow prisoner in Christ Jesus, sends you greetings. 24 And so do Mark, Aristarchus, Demas and Luke, my fellow workers. 25 The grace of the Lord Jesus Christ be with your spirit. (Philemon 1-25).

Next, A Thoughtful Examination of the Text

Paul appealed to Philemon in the way that he did because slavery was a universal practice among ancient nations and foundational to their economy. Slaves did not only menial manual labour but also often did tasks that required intelligence, artistic, musical and linguistic skills and cultural refinement. This was specially true in Greek civilization, but regardless of the nation or culture, the slave possessed no rights and was in complete subjection to his master. Paul himself was accustomed to a more humane world and he came from a scriptural educational background that had an aversion to slavery. However, he had been called to the Gentile world in order to preach the Gospel and from what he has said here and elsewhere we can see that he wisely accepted that slavery was an established institution, which if he chose to attempt to suddenly abolish it, would result in widespread insurrection and reprisals of Imperial power against the Church that would have been crippling. He was nevertheless aware of slavery abuses so what he tried to do was to instill moderation to both slaves and masters within the existing conditions. Further, Paul never hesitated to proclaim the comprehensive spiritual equality of freemen and slaves, the Christian brotherhood of men and the fatherhood of God. He wrote, "For you are all the children of God by faith in Christ Jesus. For as many of you as have been baptized in Christ, have put on Christ. There is neither Jew nor Greek, there is neither bond nor free: there is neither male nor female. For you are all one in Christ Jesus" (Galatians 3:28). These fundamental Christian principles leisurely and progressively spread throughout the whole empire. In the process they curtailed the abuses of slavery and finally destroyed it.

Like the other letters that have now become known as the prison epistles, this one was written during a time that Paul was a prisoner for the sake or cause of Christ Jesus. The letter was unmistakably from Paul himself and bore the sound of his voice. Paul's greeting was directed to Philemon of course, but also to Apphia, likely Philemon's wife and Archippus, Philemon's son, as well as to the church of believers who regularly met in Philemon's home. It was a house church. What an impact the public reading of this letter might have upon the gathering, specially if Philemon responded favourably to the request that Paul is making. It had the potential of being an exemplary statement about mercy, forgiveness and restitution.

> *1 Paul, a prisoner of Christ Jesus, and Timothy our brother, To Philemon our dear friend and fellow worker, 2 to Apphia our sister, to Archippus our fellow soldier and to the church that meets in your home: 3 Grace to you and peace from God our Father and*

the Lord Jesus Christ. (Philemon 1-3)

In verse one, Timothy is also named as a joint sender and identified as a brother. Christians were part of a spiritual family and were referred to as brothers and sisters in Christ. Paul's estimation of Philemon is that he is a fellow worker for the faith and is beloved by Paul. Fellow labourer is the Greek term synergos, from which we derive synergy. Synergy is working together. Philemon must have been earnestly involved in Paul's work for the Gospel, perhaps starting first at Ephesus where he met and knew Paul and afterwards at Colossae, his hometown. The opposite of synergy is antagonism and Paul sincerely wished to avoid that as he wrote this letter. Hopefully, Paul and Philemon could work together for a solution to Onesimus.

According to verse two, the same kind of familiarity within the family of Christ is accorded to Apphia who although she is Philemon's wife, Paul speaks of her as "our sister," because their Father in common is the LORD God. Archippus is none other than the person mentioned in Colossians 4:17. Here he is called a "fellow soldier," and in Colossians, Paul wanted him to be reminded to fulfill his ministry calling, whatever that was. The remarks in Colossians were made within a reference to the city of Laodicea and a Christian woman named Nympha whose home was used as a church, and ancient references and tradition present Archippus as a leader of that church. Clearly he did fulfill his ministry.

To all three of these people Paul commends the grace and peace of God our Father and the Lord Jesus Christ in verse three.

The Necessary Characteristics Of Someone Who Forgives

If Paul is going to ask Philemon to do what we know he will ask, Philemon needs to be a certain kind of person. Is he that kind of man? Here is what

God in the Open

Paul thinks about Philemon.

> *4 I always thank my God as I remember you in my prayers, 5 because I hear about your faith in the Lord Jesus and your love for all the saints. 6 I pray that you may be active in sharing your faith, so that you will have a full understanding of every good thing we have in Christ. 7 Your love has given me great joy and encouragement, because you, brother, have refreshed the hearts of the saints. (Philemon 4-7, NIV)*

If a person did not understand how purely motivated a man Paul was, this paragraph could be perceived as a superlative attempt at flattery for a purpose, to butter someone up, a gratuitous display of affirmations and compliments in order to lay a request on Philemon. The truth is that Paul meant every word of it. Philemon was as good a man as Paul said he was, and Paul was appealing to this quality character because of the importance of his request.

Philemon was on Paul's prayer list. Paul bathed his leaders in prayer. In verse four, the word "remember" or "mention" implies intercession. Prayer was a regular practice for Paul, a habit and Paul interceded for Philemon, which tells Philemon how highly Paul thinks of him. Each time that Paul mentions Philemon's name in prayer, Paul gives God thanks for the man. Paul sets an example continual thanksgiving and intercession to be standard for every believer. It's helpful then to have a prayer list if you haven't developed one. The reason that Paul thanks God for Philemon is stated in verse five, namely, that Paul is constantly hearing positive feedback about Philemon's character. "*I hear about your faith in the Lord Jesus and your love for all the saints.*" The man had developed the ability to connect his love and trust in Jesus Christ, with his love for and trust in other believers and their welfare.

When I read verse six, in which Paul is heard to pray for Philemon.

"I pray that you may be active in sharing your faith, so that you will have a full understanding of every good thing we have in Christ." I remember sharing my faith with a man named Jim Baldry. I was in his home and he listened eagerly, processed what he heard and then kneeled at his couch and prayed to invite Christ to become his Saviour. He then immediately stood up and said, "I have to call my mom and my brother. They need to know this." In the days that followed, he did share his faith with them and they believed. Both Jim and his brother Steve went on to train and to serve in Christian work.

It's sad but it's possible that the gospel can become dead-ended among believers, that is, the gospel stopped when it came to us. Someone shared the gospel with us and we gained assurance that our sins were forgiven and that we have an eternal hope, but we have not passed it to anyone else. Paul's prayers were determined that faith would not be dead-ended with Philemon. Paul tells Philemon that he asks God to enable Philemon to share his faith effectively. A sign of spiritual maturity is the desire to share Christ with others.

Sharing faith meant more than a simple oral gospel presentation. It also involved living his faith, demonstrating trust in God, being an example of how faith affects thinking and behaviour. I say that because the word "sharing' is the word 'fellowship'. Philemon would fellowship his faith so commendably that it would communicate to and edify everyone. We need not be natural conversationalists yet we must understand that by your life, our kindness, our friendship, our own example and testimony, we are letting people know who Jesus is. Sharing faith with others is a result of our understanding of God's provisions, which are captured in the phrase "the full knowledge," or the "acknowledgement" of what we actually have in the Christ. The more we understand that, the more eager we are to share it.

Authorities in Rome were restraining Paul. It must have been heartening to him to think of Philemon's loving treatment of him in earlier times. Philemon's love was exceptional. He tells Philemon, *"Your love has given me great joy and encouragement, because you, brother, have refreshed the hearts of the saints"* (verse 7). Paul knew that Philemon had a reputation for loving hospitality, routinely and predictably showing cordiality and affection to other believers and that is obvious from Paul's request in verse 22 that Philemon should prepare a guest room for him in the event that he can come for a visit. Mutual edification of believers is a compelling trademark of Christianity? It is an evidence of the Spirit of God. God calls us to refresh one another. You do not need to have personality plus, or be an extrovert, or super gregarious. Sometimes a drink of water is enough to refresh another Christian. May the LORD make you and me a blessing.

Paul's Appeal To Philemon

> *8 Therefore, although in Christ I could be bold and order you to do what you ought to do, 9 yet I appeal to you on the basis of love. I then, as Paul--an old man and now also a prisoner of Christ Jesus-- 10 I appeal to you for my son Onesimus, who became my son while I was in chains. (Philemon 8-10, NIV)*

Paul now arrives at the primary reason for writing the letter, that is, to acquire Philemon's forgiveness of Onesimus. Paul knew that Philemon, as a slave owner, had authority as judge, jury and possibly executioner over his slave. The slave had no rights whatsoever. Both Paul and Onesimus understood the risk Onesimus had taken in returning to his master. Paul tells Philemon that he, as Philemon's spiritual father and mentor, could reasonably order Philemon to comply. Paul doesn't lack the courage to do that but he chooses not to take that approach. It is not always wise to use authority to make a point to achieve an objective. It's better to ask God for discernment and wisdom to distinguish the best courses of action. Paul can't force Philemon to do anything. Besides, he possesses little leverage when he by admission is a senior and presently a prisoner without access to Philemon. So, in verses 9 and 10 we hear Paul choosing rather to use their mutual love as the foundation for his request. "For love's sake, by reason of your love for me and my love for you and my love for Onesimus," Paul asserts, "I am appealing to you for Onesimus who is like a son to me now. I adopted him when he showed up during my imprisonment. He has been of no value to you for some time, but now has become profitable to both you and me." Love always moves relational mountains and barriers better than coercion does.

Paul's Motives For Asking

> *11 Formerly he was useless to you, but now he has become useful both to you and to me. 12 I am sending him--who is my very heart--back to you. 13 I would have liked to keep him with me so that he could take your place in helping me while I am in chains for the gospel. 14 But I did not want to do anything without your consent, so that any favor you do will be spontaneous and not forced. 15 Perhaps the reason he was separated from you for a little while was that you might have him back for good-- 16 no longer as a slave, but better than a slave, as a dear brother. He is very dear to me but even dearer to you, both as a man and as a brother in the Lord. (Philemon 11-16, NIV)*

I love Paul's play on the name of Onesimus, which actually means "useful." He has been useless to Philemon but Onesimus is going to live up to his name, 'useful'. Paul is admitting that Philemon has a legitimate case against Onesimus. Onesimus has been unprofitable, virtually useless to Philemon. In fact in verse 18, Paul later offers that if there is any outstanding debt or money owed, or if Onesimus had wronged Philemon,

Paul would cover those costs. That is an acknowledgment that the slave stole from his master. Even if all that is meant is that because of his flight, Onesimus proved not to be a good business deal for his master because he was unavailable and therefore useless, Paul will be good for that cost. But Paul immediately makes the promise that Onesimus will be useful to you again and to me as well because I am sending him back to you. That's how radically God's grace transforms a person. Paul wants Philemon to understand that this man has had a faith encounter with Jesus Christ and that never happens without turning a person's life right around. Paul has given Onesimus his stamp of approval. That should mean something to Philemon. Philemon must have been impressed that Onesimus had actually returned to him to bear whatever the consequences might be. Only Jesus could make a man so responsible, concerned about integrity and making restitution.

Verse 13 is an evident endorsement of Onesimus by Paul who would have wanted nothing more than to keep Onesimus in Rome with him to assist him to do gospel work when he himself was limited by his imprisonment. Onesimus could fulfill logistical and practical needs. I don't think Paul could make it any clearer how necessary it was for Paul to have the help of other people, and how profitable it would be for Onesimus to be returned to Paul. Something that we may not have known but Paul surely would have known, was that according to Old Testament law, Jews were obliged to provide asylum to fugitive slaves. Deuteronomy 23:15-16 says, *"You shall not hand over to his master a slave who has escaped from his master to you. He shall live with you in your midst, in the place which he shall choose in one of your towns where it pleases him; you shall not mistreat him."* Paul could have satisfied his own conscience to keep Onesimus, but in verse 14 Paul asserts that he would refuse to presume upon Philemon's graciousness, and he would not use his instrumentality in Philemon's salvation as a power play. The last thing Paul wants in this situation is for Philemon to do something against his will and out of obligation. He wants Philemon to make a sincere well-considered voluntary choice to grant Paul's request. That's impressive and good leadership that appeals to volition rather than imposition.

I myself would never endorse slavery. I still find it reprehensible that slavery existed so recently in American history and furthermore that African Americans had to wait until Presidents Kennedy and Johnson to enjoy equal human and civic rights. Of course I understand that slavery was culturally acceptable in Paul's day. Looking at it like that, the escape of a slave was regarded not as a good and liberating event but as a bad and troublesome action. And since that is the way Philemon regarded it, Paul was trying to help him to see that perhaps God turned evil into good. I love the theological logic Paul used here. God used the escape of a renegade slave to accomplish his purpose. "**15** Perhaps the reason he was separated from you for a little while was that you might have him back for good-- **16** no longer as a slave, but better than a slave, as a dear brother. He is very dear to me but even dearer to you, both as a man and as a brother in the Lord."

The slave's thievery and flight to Rome led to his salvation and to him becoming a better employee for Philemon, but more importantly he could now be regarded as a much loved brother. You will have him back forever. Paul says he himself regards Onesimus as a brother and Philemon has that much more reason to look at him that way, as a fellow man and as a brother in the Lord.

That last phrase is the reason why some speculate that perhaps

Onesimus was actually Philemon's own blood brother, and through some financial setback, whether bad business, or gambling, Onesimus was obliged to assign himself to his brother in servitude. That was sometimes done in those years. I don't buy it in this case, because if this sibling relationship had existed, much more would have been made of it to make sense of the story. Paul is at least arguing that Onesimus' spiritual status transcends their social distinctions. Both are brothers in Christ and that supersedes slave and master.

Paul's Summary Request for Philemon to Accept Onesimus

17 So if you consider me a partner, welcome him as you would welcome me.

This verse is the consequent follow through of the previous statements. Paul makes a plea on the basis of his partnership and fellowship in the Lord with Philemon. He asks that Philemon will receive Onesimus as readily and warmly as he would receive Paul himself.

Paul's offer to Cover Outstanding Debt

18 If he has done you any wrong or owes you anything, charge it to me. 19 I, Paul, am writing this with my own hand. I will pay it back--not to mention that you owe me your very self. 20 I do wish, brother, that I may have some benefit from you in the Lord; refresh my heart in Christ. (Philemon 18-20, NIV)

Paul is essentially endorsing a promissory note. He is willing to pay the price for Onesimus' guilt. Jesus did the same thing for Paul and for Philemon. Grace gives as grace receives. Paul asks Philemon to charge him with any financial loss Philemon may have incurred. Put it on my charge account he says. And Paul's quick mention of his own handwriting of this document is a way of saying that his word makes this a legal and binding document as far as his last comment is concerned. Paul doesn't care about the cost, but I get a kick out of what looks like a jab but is a heartfelt reminder that Philemon owed a debt to Paul. He said, *"...I will pay it back--not to mention that you owe me your very self."* Philemon was a man to whom Onesimus owed a debt but Philemon owed a debt as well and Philemon's debt was greater than Onesimus' debt, his salvation. His was an eternal debt to God. He owed a debt to Paul for sharing the gospel with Onesimus who is now a changed man, so Philemon had a double debt. As diplomatic and tactfully correct as Paul has tried to be, he is unarguably direct when he needs to be. He wants a 'yes' response. If Philemon frees Onesimus then Paul will have joy. He is basically saying, "*If you deal kindly with him you will bless me, refresh me, he is saying. As a brother in Christ, I expect this from you.*"

Paul's confidence that Philemon will Emancipate Onesimus

21 Confident of your obedience, I write to you, knowing that you will do even more than I ask.

Grace transcends obligation and necessity and is generous and extensive. Paul is expressing confidence in the outcome although there is not biblical statement that reveals to us, Philemon's reaction to Paul's letter. Did he take advantage of the Roman laws that would permit him to punish severely, even with death? Or, did he set Onesimus free? Did Onesimus return to his position as slave, but with the fellowship of his newfound brothers and sisters in Christ? There are several possibilities.

Paul asks Philemon to pray that the Roman government will release Paul and that he may visit Colossae, and anticipating that, he asks in advance for lodging.

22 And one thing more: Prepare a guest room for me, because I hope to be restored to you in answer to your prayers.

God in the Open

Paul then signs off with further greetings from fellow workers familiar to Philemon and who are presently with Paul in Rome. He concludes with a final benediction.

> **23** *Epaphras, my fellow prisoner in Christ Jesus, sends you greetings.* **24** *And so do Mark, Aristarchus, Demas and Luke, my fellow workers.* **25** *The grace of the Lord Jesus Christ be with your spirit. (Philemon 23-25, NIV).*

The Legacy of Onesimus

We can't come to a firm conclusion as to what happened to Onesimus. At the end of Colossians, we read that Tychicus and Onesimus carried the letter from Paul to the Colossian church. If Philemon was written first and the Colossian letter came later, that would suggest that Onesimus had been set free and had become part of Paul's ministry team. That may be stretching probability because the distance between Rome and Colossae was so great that the two letters were likely carried at the same time.

Another factor to inform us emerges from the writings of Ignatius, a church father forty years after the Philemon letter was written. He wrote a series of letters to churches in Asia Minor, letters that still survive today and in one of those he has written to the church in Ephesus, addressing the bishop of Ephesus named Onesimus. Onesimus was a common name but it was mostly applied to slaves. What are the chances that a bishop would be named Onesimus, unless it's the man we meet here?

These next thoughts are convincing to me. The letter of Philemon exists and is included in the canon of inspired scripture. Why? If Philemon had rejected Paul's request to accept Onesimus back as a brother, would this letter have continued to exist? Would it have been copied and circulated? That's not very likely. If the situation ended poorly, why would anyone keep it? I believe this story had a happy ending. The evidence points to it. The letter would be copied by a house church and distributed because the outcome was precisely what Paul had wanted. Philemon granted Paul's wish. Beyond that we cannot be certain. Was he fully emancipated? Was he set free to return to help Paul? Was he kept on as a slave but with a very different relationship than previously? We can't know but we have enough evidence to conclude that he was better off because Paul wrote the letter. Ignatius wrote: "Onesimus by name, Onesimus by nature." He was useful by name and by nature.

About the Author

Ron Unruh holds a D.Min. from Trinity Evangelical Divinity School of Deerfield, Illinois. Over a forty-year period he pastored four churches; was an occasional adjunct instructor in homiletics at Northwest Baptist College, Langley B.C., and Tyndale University College and Seminary, Toronto ON; and served as President of the Evangelical Free Church of Canada. He resides in British Columbia where he writes and paints and regularly drives an MX5 soft-top sports car to saltwater at Crescent Beach and White Rock Beach.

ISBN 978-0-9939342-0-9

Look for Ron's other titles such as the children's novel 'Crandall's Door', and 'The Eleven' My Interviews with the Apostles, Narratives and Nurture.

www.ingramcontent.com/pod-product-compliance
Lightning Source LLC
Chambersburg PA
CBHW071005160426
43193CB00012B/1920